The LMIII Cemetery at Tourloti, Siteia

The 'Xanthoudidis Master' and the Octopus Style in East Crete

Constantinos Paschalidis

with a contribution by

P. J. P. McGeorge

BAR International Series 1917
2009

Published in 2016 by
BAR Publishing, Oxford

BAR International Series 1917

The LMIII Cemetery at Tourloti, Siteia

© The authors individually and the Publisher 2009

The authors' moral rights under the 1988 UK Copyright,
Designs and Patents Act are hereby expressly asserted.

All rights reserved. No part of this work may be copied, reproduced, stored,
sold, distributed, scanned, saved in any form of digital format or transmitted
in any form digitally, without the written permission of the Publisher.

ISBN 9781407304007 paperback
ISBN 9781407334295 e-format
DOI https://doi.org/10.30861/9781407304007
A catalogue record for this book is available from the British Library

BAR Publishing is the trading name of British Archaeological Reports (Oxford) Ltd.
British Archaeological Reports was first incorporated in 1974 to publish the BAR
Series, International and British. In 1992 Hadrian Books Ltd became part of the BAR
group. This volume was originally published by Archaeopress in conjunction with
British Archaeological Reports (Oxford) Ltd / Hadrian Books Ltd, the Series principal
publisher, in 2009. This present volume is published by BAR Publishing, 2016.

BAR titles are available from:

	BAR Publishing
	122 Banbury Rd, Oxford, OX2 7BP, UK
EMAIL	info@barpublishing.com
PHONE	+44 (0)1865 310431
FAX	+44 (0)1865 316916
	www.barpublishing.com

TABLE OF CONTENTS

Acknowledgements 2

Chapter I: The LMIII Cemetery at Tourloti, Siteia 3

    The Chamber Tomb Excavated by Metaxia Tsipopoulou 5

    The Chamber Tomb Excavated by Nikos Papadakis 10

    The Vases Presented by Manolis Fygetakis 21

    Conclusions: Tourloti in the LMIII Period 27

Appendix: The Trefoil Spouted Jugs 14624, 14625 and 14626 of the National Archaeological Museum   29

Chapter II: Stirrup-jar SM 4026, the 'Xanthoudidis Master', and the Octopus Style in East Crete   30

Chapter III (by P.J.P. McGeorge): The Cremation Burial from Plakalona, Tourloti 37

Summary (Περίληψη) 42

Summary (Estratto) 44

Abbreviations – Bibliography 45

List of Plates and Figures 56

Acknowledgements

The subject of the present study was initially suggested to me by Dr Metaxia Tsipopoulou, now Director of the National Archive of Monuments, who offered her encouragement and entrusted me with the material from her excavations at Tourloti; to her I owe my deepest gratitude.

I wish to express my warmest thanks to the Director of the 24th Ephorate of Prehistoric and Classical Antiquities (East Crete), Ms Vili Apostolakou and to archaeologist, Ms Chryssa Sofianou, who issued the permit to study and publish the material from the excavations of the late Ephor Nikos Papadakis and the group of vases presented to the Museum by Manolis Fygetakis. I also owe many thanks to Dr Lena Papazoglou-Manioudaki, Head of the Prehistoric Collection of the National Archaeological Museum at Athens, who allowed me to publish the trefoil spouted jugs, NAM 14624, 14625 and 14626 from the Minoan Collection of the Museum. Photographs of these three vases by Ms Irini Kapiri were offered to me by Ms Eleni Morati, Head of the Photographic Archive of the Museum; I am indebted to both these colleagues. I owe my gratitude to Professor Nikolaos Stampolidis, Director of the Museum of Cycladic Art (N.P. Goulandris Foundation) and to the curator, Dr Nikolas Papadimitriou, who allowed me to study, draw and present the stirrup-jar CAM 484.

Professor Andreas Vlachopoulos contributed much with his comments on the final text and gave me permission to reproduce the drawing and photographs of the stirrup-jar NM 914 from Aplomata, Naxos. Dr Colin Macdonald generously gave me the photographs of the Mouliana stirrup-jars from his personal archive and assisted me in various stages of this work. Drs Birgitta Hallager, Eleni Konstantinidi, Eleni Hatzaki and Penelope Mountjoy shared with me various ideas and thoughts. Dr Eleni Farmakidou, archaeologist of the 22nd Ephorate of Prehistoric and Classical Antiquities (Rhodes), provided me with the photographs of the two stirrup-jars from Ialysos published in this volume, while Ms Ioanna Ninou, Head of the Photographic Archive of the Athens Archaeological Society gave me permission to reproduce the drawings of the two Octopus Style stirrup-jars from Mouliana. Dr Angelo Lui on behalf of the Photographic Service of the Musée d' Art et d' Histoire, Ville de Genève, provided me with the photograph of the Minoan larnax inv.n.23436. Ms Amalia Kakissis, archivist of the British School at Athens, allowed me to reproduce the photograph of a stirrup-jar from Vassiliki, Ierapera, illustrated in BSA vol. 62. Drs Leslie Preston Day and Anna-Lucia D'Agata allowed me to reproduce drawings of some published Close Octopus Style stirrup-jars from their excavations. Professor Maria Xanthopoulou translated the first two Chapters from Greek into fluent English and Mr Paolo Daniele Scirpo translated the Greek summary into Italian. Ms Kleio Zervaki provided me with the photograph of the village of Tourloti, illustrated in plate 1. Mr Nikos Papadopoulos and Mr Vangelis Tsingiaouroglou provided generously their technical advice and support in various stages of this work. I am deeply indebted to all the above.

Finally, I am much obliged to Mr Manolis Kafkalakis and Ms Euterpe Triantafyllou, guards of the Siteia Archaeological Museum, for their warm hospitality and help during my study there in the summers of 2003 and 2007.

Mr Chronis Papanikolopoulos, photographer of the INSTAP Center in East Crete, took the photographs of the skeletal remains, while the author drew and photographed all the Tourloti vases and small finds. The author also made the drawings of the stirrup-jar CAM 484, while Dr Metaxia Tsipopoulou drew the plan of the chamber tomb illustrated in figure 2.

Chapter I

THE LMIII CEMETERY AT TOURLOTI, SITEIA

Halfway along the mountainous route between the Ierapetra isthmus and Siteia, on the northern limits of the western mountain range of the Siteia province, is the small village of Tourloti (**pl. 1a**).[1] Approximately 2.5 kilometres north of the village, on the hillside that drops down to the beach at Mochlos, on the site of Plakalona, is a LMIII chamber tomb cemetery. Richard B. Seager was the first to identify and excavate the site in 1900.[2] He collected the LMIII stirrup-jar now in the museum of the University of Pennsylvania.[3] In 1906, Stefanos Xanthoudidis reported that 'Mycenaean' copper alloy weapons and tools had been found – exactly when is unknown – at Metochia, Tourloti.[4] In 1910, Angelo Mosso mentioned the existence of a bronze 'Mycenaean' knife from Tourloti and presented the results of its chemical analysis[5]. The first brief archaeological report for investigations in the area was published in 1938 by Manolis Mavroreidis of Siteia, temporary curator of antiquities and schoolteacher, who excavated a rich grave at Plakalona, unpublished to this day (**fig. 1**).[6] In 1959, Nikolaos Platon identified a further group of rock-hewn chamber tombs, which he never excavated, despite his original intentions.[7]

The chance discovery of seven vases from one or more tombs at the end of the 1950's or the beginning of the 1960's once again disturbed the cemetery's eternal peace (**pl. 2a**). The circumstances of this discovery are unknown, though the tombs were probably identified and disturbed during agricultural work. The vases were presented to the Archaeological Service by Manolis Fygetakis of Siteia.[8] Fygetakis also handed in a LMIIIC tub larnax from the same cemetery. The larnax's publication by Metaxia Tsipopoulou and Lucia Vagnetti is the only thorough study of any find from this site.[9] An undecorated LMIIIC

---

[1] For a brief historical review of Tourloti from antiquity until modern times see Papadakis 1983 128-129. Succinct information on the archaeology of the wider area of Tourloti is included in the catalogues by Pendlebury 1963, 236, 237, 266; Pini 1968, 92, n. 13; Leekley and Noyes 1975, 69; Kanta 1980, 173; Löwe 1996, 164-165; Effinger 1996, 306.

[2] Although Seager does not specify the exact spot of his discovery, he refers to a site "directly below Tourloti", which can probably be identified as Plakalona, located on the north slope of the hill on which the village is built, see Seager 1909, 286.

[3] Seager mentions finding the Octopus Style stirrup-jar, now in Pennsylvania, during his short excavation at the Tourloti cemetery, which he did not publish, see Betancourt 1983, 52, fig. 14 and pl. 12 (n. 137).

[4] Xanthoudidis 1906, 135 referred succinctly to a bronze spear, some axes and a few daggers from Metochia, Tourloti as parallels to similar finds from Chamezi, Siteia. Hood and de Jong 1952, 261 n.104 mentioned the existence of the same "LM hoard of bronzes from Tourloti" in Herakleion Museum. In particular, they reported the inventory number of the sole spear from this context: HM 542. Höckmann 1980, 15-16, 130 cat.n.A5 included this very same spear in his typology, as an example of 'type A', but he quoted by mistake "Xenaki 1950, 261 no picture" istead of "Hood and de Jong 1952, 261 no picture". A double axe from the same group of bronzes is illustrated in Montelius 1924, pl.5:11a-b (inv.n. HM 535), while all double axes are published in Buchholz 1959, 44 cat.n. 34, 38 (inv.n. HM 533-537). Finally, a chisel, a knife and a sickle from this group were published by Deshayes 1960 vol.I, 88-89 cat.n.733 (HM 539), 352 cat.n.2849 (HM 541) and vol. II, 38 cat.n.733 (HM 539), 151 cat.n.2849 (HM 541) and pls.47:16 and 62:9.

[5] Mosso 1910, 308, and Deshayes 1960, vol. II, 139, n. 2652, who dated it to the LMIII period or the fourteenth – thirteenth centuries BC.

[6] Mavroeidis 1938, 218, where some of the tomb's finds are pictured, and 219, where the author briefly describes the tomb and lists its finds. The complete lack of pottery or other large finds suggests that the tomb had been looted in antiquity. The numerous stone, glass, and faience beads and animal shaped small finds, the "twelve sardonyx seal stones", and the copper-alloy jewellery and small tools were obviously overlooked by the grave robbers. These finds remain unpublished.

[7] Platon 1959a, 388-389. From the following year onwards, Platon's interest must have concentrated on the major discovery of the Zakros palace, see Platon and Davaras 1960, 526.

[8] The Siteia Museum inventory mentions the submission by Fygetakis of seven vases from the site of "Plakalona-Linaras", but without a date (year). The vases were probably handed over between 1958 and 1962, when Fygetakis showed Platon many previously unknown archaeological sites in the Siteia province and supplied the Agios Nikolaos Archaeological Museum with "numerous chance finds from East Crete", see Platon 1959, 219; Platon 1959a, 389; Platon 1960, 307; Platon and Davaras 1960, 526. Unfortunately, nothing is known of the type of grave or graves in which the vases were found.

[9] Tsipopoulou and Vagnetti 1999, 124. The authors mention Fygetakis presenting the larnax to the Agios Nikolaos Archaeological Museum, without any further information on the precise time and place of its discovery.

stirrup-jar from the cemetery is now in the Herakleion Museum.[10]

In June 1984, after the Town of Tourloti notified the Archaeological Service of antiquities found during construction work, Metaxia Tsipopoulou excavated a looted chamber tomb at Plakalona,[11] and Nikos Papadakis investigated a second, richly appointed chamber tomb.[12] A third looted LMIII chamber tomb was identified in 1990.[13] Finally, in 2006, Vassiliki Zografaki, curator of antiquities, excavated another wealthy chamber tomb.

This work presents the finds of the chamber tombs excavated by Tsipopoulou **(pl. 2b)** and Papadakis **(pl. 1b)**, and the vases handed over by Fygetakis **(pl. 2a)**. The Fygetakis group includes Octopus Close Style stirrup-jar SM 4026 **(pls. 4a, 4b and figs. 48-53)**, presented in the volume's second chapter together with a discussion of its attribution to a particular workshop and a distinct vase painter conventionally dubbed the 'Xanthoudidis Master'. In the absence of petrographic or other analysis,[14] any hypothesis on the vase's provenance is based on morphological and stylistic criteria, and on the fabric's macroscopic examination.

The vases excavated by Tsipopoulou and Papadakis are on display in the Siteia Archaeological Museum (Case 9). Those presented by Fygetakis are kept in the storerooms of the same museum. A study of the human bones from the Papadakis excavation by Dr Photini J. P. McGeorge completes this volume.[15]

---

[10] Kanta 1980, 173 and fig. 66:9. The precise time and place of the vase's discovery are not mentioned.
[11] Tsipopoulou 1995, 186.
[12] Papadakis 1984, 306.
[13] Pariente 1991, 939; French 1991-1992, 69, where the discovery of a small, looted chamber tomb containing LMIII pottery is mentioned briefly. The *Archeologikon Deltion (Chronika)* for that year, however, mentions no such find.
[14] Sampling intact vases for any sort of analysis is not feasible because of the destruction it would entail.
[15] Despite the efforts of the Siteia Museum guards, no other skeletal remains from these two tombs were identified inside the storerooms.

THE CHAMBER TOMB EXCAVATED BY METAXIA TSIPOPOULOU

The chamber tomb excavated by Metaxia Tsipopoulou had a roughly circular shape (max. diameter: 1.9, min. diameter: 1.5) with a shallow niche on one side (**fig. 2**).[16] Its rock-hewn dromos was completely destroyed by the mechanical excavator, and only the dry-stone wall of the opening was preserved intact. The tomb was excavated from the chamber's roof, which had already fallen in antiquity and formed an irregular dome with converging walls preserved to a height of 1.25 m.

The tomb was looted, probably after its roof collapsed, as indicated by the scant skeletal remains and potsherds, scattered throughout the backfill over the floor. Of the tomb's original contents, only two groups of objects were found next to the north wall. The first group, which occupied a small part of the main chamber and a shallow niche, 0.40 m deep and 0.70 m wide, comprised two vases (SM 4511 and SM 4512) and the bones from a secondary burial of a single individual. The second group, which occupied an area 0.50x0.40 m along the north wall, between the first group and the chamber's opening, also included the bones of a secondary burial. The disturbed backfill over the rest of the floor contained twelve, mostly non-joining, sherds from various vases, a clay biconical spindle whorl, and a few broken bones, all from the grave gifts and burials that were disturbed by the grave robbers.

The tomb's architectural type, which features a roughly circular or elliptical chamber, with an average diameter of 1.5-3 m, a domed roof, a relatively short dromos, and a dry stone wall blocking the opening, is the most common type in Crete in the LMIII period. In East Crete, similar tombs have been identified at Mochlos,[17] Pachyammos,[18] Gra Lygia in Ierapetra,[19] Farmakokefalo near Sklavoi,[20] etc. The other two graves excavated by Emmanouil Mavroeidis[21] and Nikos Papadakis at Tourloti, and the many looted graves now gaping at Plakalona have a similar shape and size.

Of the few finds excavated by Tsipopoulou we present here a three-handled piriform jar or small krater (SM 4511) and a trefoil spouted jug (SM 4512) (**pl. 2b**). The clay biconical spindle whorl (SM 4532), the twelve pottery sherds from cups, piriform jars, stirrup-jars, and tripod vessels (SM 4532-4543), and the skeletal remains collected during the excavation were not found.

SM 4511. Three-handled piriform jar or small krater (FS 44, **figs. 3-4**). Complete. Small chips on the entire body and concretions in places, particularly on the lower part. Fine, yellowish-brown clay, uniform slip, black, glossy paint, fugitive in places. Wide cylindrical neck ending in a flat, slightly oblique, flaring rim. Horizontal strap handles on the shoulder. Piriform body, tall biconical foot. Neck and rim monochrome painted throughout. Handles monochrome painted on the top and sides. Three bands of dense painted decoration on the shoulder. The upper, narrower band consists of a row of N-pattern (FM 60:1), the middle band of leaves ('foliate band', FM 64:14), and the lower band of a zigzag combined with parallel angles and dotted or empty lozenges ('Minoan iris', FM 10A:g). Directly below the shoulder, a group of six parallel bands runs across the top of the belly; four more bands decorate its bottom. The foot is monochrome. A painted ring runs around the base disk, where the potter's string mark is visible. Slipped interior, with traces of the potter's wheel.

Height: 16 cm, rim diameter: 10.3 cm, maximum diameter: 13.7 cm, base diameter: 5.6 cm.

The shape of the small LH/LMIII piriform jar or krater comes from the large piriform jars of the Minoan Palatial Style.[22] The Tourloti vase (SM 4511) reproduces Furumark's Shape 44 (small piriform jar), known from numerous Mycenaean examples dating from the LHIIIA1 until the early LHIIIA2 period.[23] The LMIIIA variant features a broad, tall, cylindrical, often monochrome painted neck, which distinguishes it from other Helladic vases.[24] Its decoration usually consists of a broad

---

[16] Tsipopoulou 1995, 186.
[17] Soles and Davaras 1996, 211-222 and fig. 18. Also see Soles and Davaras 2008, 130.
[18] Alexiou 1954, 399-400 fig. 1; Alexiou and Davaras 1964, 441.
[19] Apostolakou 1998, 26, 28 drawing 3, 29-30 and drawing 4.
[20] Alexiou and Davaras 1964, 442-443.
[21] Mavroeidis 1938, 219.

[22] Furumark 1941, 24-29, 101; Kanta 1980, 276.
[23] Furumark 1941, 23, fig. 4, 591; Mountjoy 1994, 60-61, fig. 62 (LHIIIA1).
[24] Kanta 1980, 276.

decorative zone on the shoulder and parallel bands lower on the body.[25] Similar vases were found in graves at Knossos,[26] Myrsini,[27] Farmakokefalo-Sklavoi,[28] Karpathos,[29] and elsewhere. One vase from Farmakokephalo-Sklavoi recalls the shape and secondary decoration of the Tourloti vase so closely that it may come from the same workshop.[30]

The decoration of the Tourloti vase (parallel rows of N-pattern, foliate bands and zigzags combined with Minoan irises) is common throughout the LMII, LMIIIA1 periods and until the early LMIIIA2 period[31] on various open and closed shapes throughout Crete[32] and in the Dodecanese.[33] On the Greek mainland, this combination of motifs is unusual and occurs only on a few imported Minoan vases, such as the famous LMIIIA1 Knossian jug from Grave 24 at Prosymna.[34] Another piriform jar from Grave 6 at Zafer Papoura, with the same combination of decorative motifs on the shoulder, probably comes from the same Knossian workshop as the Prosymna jug.[35]

The piriform jar from Tourloti is made in a fine, yellowish-brown fabric and features a uniform slip and glossy black paint, all of which are characteristic of Knossian wares.[36] Moreover, it closely resembles, both in shape and decoration, the above-mentioned piriform jar from Zafer Papoura. The obvious difference between the Tourloti vase and both its contemporary, somewhat 'heavier' shapes of East Cretan amphorae, such as those of Gra Lygia[37] and Farmakokefalo,[38] and the East Cretan imitations of Knossian models,[39] strongly suggest that it was made at Knossos, either at the end of the LMIIIA1 period or in the early LMIIIA2 period.

SM 4512. Trefoil spouted jug (**figs. 5-7**). Complete. Small chip at the edge of the spout, larger chip on the belly. White concretions in places. Traces of a calcified woven fabric visible on a patch of concretions at the widest point. Fine, pink fabric. Reddish-pink paint, fugitive in places, orange slip. Narrow, cylindrical neck ending in a simple flaring rim and trefoil spout. Handle elliptical-circular in section, attached at the rim and bottom of the shoulder. Piriform-globular body. Flat base with traces of the potter's string mark. Upper part of the vase monochrome painted, from inside the rim to the bottom of the shoulder; single drip runs the side of the belly. Some carelessly applied paint on the

---

[25] Kanta 1980, 278.

[26] Evans 1906, 27, fig. 23, from Tomb 7 at Zafer Papoura (LMIIIA1); Evans 1914, 19-20, fig. 29, from Tomb 4 of the Double Axe Tomb group (LMIIIA2).

[27] Daux 1960, 820, fig. 2 upper row, second from last (LMIIIA2).

[28] Kanta 1980, 183-184, fig. 74, 75, 76:2/7 (LMIIIA).

[29] Melas 1985, 52, pl. 64:34, from Anemomyloi, Karpathos (LMIIIA2).

[30] Kanta 1980, fig. 76:7 (LMIIIA).

[31] Popham 1970, 99, pl. 9d-f, 11b-c; Kanta 1980, 151, 278; Furumark 1941, 182.

[32] For examples of this decoration see Popham 1970, 97 fig. 3:1, 105:1-7, pl. 13:a-b, from the Royal Villa at Knossos (LMIIIA1); Popham 1984, pl. 50:a, 116:c, 177:a, from the Unexplored Mansion at Knossos (LMII and LMIIIA1); Mountjoy 2003, 130-131 fig. 4.35, n. 607, from the South House at Knossos (LMIIIA1); Hatzaki 2005, 154-155, fig. 4.20:8, n. 197, 159-160, fig. 4.23:10, n. 243, 170-171, fig. 4.29:2, n. 310, 170, 172, fig. 4.30:1, n. 321, from the Little Palace at Knossos (LMII and LMIIIA1); Warren 1997, 162, fig. 12 (second row on the right), from the excavations for the extension of the Knossos Stratigraphical Museum (LMIIIA1); Banou and Rethemiotakis 1997, 33 fig. 10:3, from Kyra Limaniotissa in Herakleion (LMIIIA1-2); Watrous 1992, 29, fig. 23, n. 500, from Kommos (LMIIIA1); Rutter and Van de Moortel 2006, 524, 1152, pl. 3.59, n. 56b/1, from the Southern Area of Kommos (LMIIIA2); Hallager and McGeorge 1992, 19, 20, pl. 19A, n. P6343, from Tomb 11 on Palamas Street in Chania (LMIIIA2); Tzedakis 1969, 397 fig. 3, from Kastelli in Chania (LMIIIA); Apostolakou 1998, 48-49, drawing 30, n. AE 12683, from Gra Lygia, Ierapetra (LMIIIA2); Banou 2005, 160, 162 fig. 17, from Mochlos (LMIIIA); Kanta 1980, 51, fig. 23:3, from Malia (LMIIIA2); 151, fig. 107:4, from Episkopi in Ierapetra (LMIIIA1); 165, fig. 108:1, from Myrsini (LMIIIA1); Tsipopoulou 1997, 224-225, fig. 21 n. 92.904, from Petras (LMIIIA1-2); Bosanquet and Dawkins 1923, 79, fig. 63, from Palaikastro (LMIIIA1).

[33] Melas 1985, 51, 53, pl. 63:12, pl. 66:45, from Karpathos (LMIIIA1-2).

[34] Blegen 1937, 84, 440, fig. 174 and 700, n. 304, from Grave XIV. Kim Shelton (1996, 56-57, 205) does not identify the jug as Minoan and dates it to the LHIIIA2 period. By contrast, Mervyn Popham (1970, 83; 1994, 99, pl. 11c), Athanasia Kanta (1980, 298), and Penelope Mountjoy (1993, 13, 14 fig. 7) consider jug 304 from Prosymna beyond doubt a Knossian LMIIIA1 product.

[35] Evans 1906, 24, 123, fig. 117:6a; Hatzaki 2007, 216-217, fig. 6.13:4, where the piriform jar from Zafer Papoura is dated to the LMIIIA1 period.

[36] Kanta 1980, 288.

[37] Apostolakou 1998, 78, drawing 55, n. AE 12724 (LMIIIA2).

[38] Kanta 1980, fig. 74:3-4, 75:1-5.

[39] Kanta 1980, fig. 74:6, 75:6. The latter example is distinguished by the tendency to imitate both the shape and the decorative scheme of the Tourloti (SM 4511) and Zafer Papoura piriform jars.

base. Traces of the potter's wheel inside the neck. Potter's fingerprints just above the base.

Height: 13 cm, maximum diameter: 11.1 cm, base diameter: 4.4 cm.

One-handled, beak-spouted jugs in an orange-red fabric, with monochrome painted rim (interior and exterior) or upper part of the body, and with drips, or irregular monochrome discs, or random brush marks on the body, form a large group of vases made in Palaikastro and widely distributed throughout East Crete in the LMIIIA1-2 periods.[40] A smaller group, closely related to the previous one, comprises piriform/globular trefoil jugs in a similar fabric, with monochrome painted rim, neck, handle and the upper part of the shoulder. Such vases have been found in wells 605 and 576 at area 6 of Palaikastro dated to the LM IB-II and LM IIIA1 respectively[41]. Very similar to this type of trefoil jugs is the type with monochrome painted upper half of the vase and a single drip on the unpainted belly, directly below the base of the handle. Such vases have been found at Myrsini, Mochlos, and Gournia[42] and are dated mainly to the LMIIIA2 period.[43] The Tourloti jug (SM 4512) was found halfway between each of these three sites. It differs from the Myrsini and Gournia jugs only in that the drip runs down the vase's side instead of back. The close similarity between the Myrsini, Mochlos, Gournia, and Tourloti jugs and the proximity of these four sites to one another suggest a common origin from a local workshop[44]. This workshop seems to have developed an older vase form, typical of the Palaikastro pottery tradition.

Three similar, unprovenanced, and unpublished trefoil-spouted jugs are kept in the Minoan Collection of the National Archaeological Museum **(figs. 43-47)**.[45] Their fabric and size resembles those of the Tourloti jug, and all of them feature a single drip under the base of the handle, just like the Myrsini and Gournia jugs. The jugs of the National Archaeological Museum can be securely attributed to the same workshop, which was active in the region between Myrsini-Tourloti and Gournia in the LMIIIA period. These three vases are presented in the *appendix*, at the end of Chapter 1.

The calcified remains of a fine textile are visible on the belly of the Tourloti jug (SM 4512) **(fig. 7)**. The location of the remains suggests that the fabric originally covered the entire vase, which was thus carefully placed as a grave gift inside the tomb. The practice of placing vases and other grave gifts wrapped in fabric inside the tombs of the prehistoric Aegean in known from a MHIII burial in Grave B of Grave Circle B at Mycenae,[46] the LHIIB/IIIA1 'Andronianoi Hoard' from Euboea,[47]

---

[40] The so-called 'domestic ware with blot and trickle decoration', known from the 'Bathroom' in Block *Gamma*, see Bosanquet and Dawkins 1923, 111-112, fig. 96:b-c; MacGillivray 1997a, 277, Tsipopoulou 1997, 249, fig. 43b; Apostolakou 1998, 54, drawing 35; Kanta 1980, 165, 262. Also see MacGillivray 1997, 198-200, fig. 3 and MacGillivray, Sackett and Driessen 2007, 146-152, where the fabric, slip, and paint of the LMIII Palaikastro ceramics and the local pottery's decorative styles are discussed.
[41] MacGillivray, Sackett and Driessen 2007, 101, 102 nos. 421 and 422 (well 605, deposit 1, LM IB), 109, 110 n. 447 (well 605, deposit 2, LM IB-II); Hatzaki 2007a, 51, 53, 54, 56 nos. 172, 177 and 178 (well 576, deposit 6b, LM IIIA1), 87.
[42] Kanta 1980, 166, fig. 109:4, n. ANM 1889. This type of trefoil-spouted jug abounds in the LMIIIA-B tombs at Mochlos and Myrsini, see Smith 2002, 187-188, 452 (P 2661), 465 (P 1199), 470 (P 1521, P 1548), 473 (P 1459), 474 (P 1536), 487 (SM 11112, SM 11113), 493 (SM 11117), 495 (SM 11118), 498 (SM 11068), 502 (SM 11129) from the cemetery of Mochlos and Smith 2002, 515 (ANM 1889), 526 (ANM 1921), 528 (SM 3518), 536 (ANM 1963), 541 (SM 3523) from the cemetery of Myrsini. See also Smith 2004, 313-314 and fig.22.7; Smith 2005, 191, 192, fig. 5 (right), 197, fig. 8 (back left); Banou 2005, 160; Soles and Davaras 2008, pl. 29D (above left), pl. 30C (above right), pl. 37B (right), pl. 38C (left).

[43] Smith 2002, 188-189. The only possible comparison with a LHIIIA2 pottery shape is with the squat jug FS 114, which is usually monochrome and has the lip slightly pinched-out opposite the handle, see Furumark 1941, 84, 602:114.
[44] Tsipopoulou supports the existence of an important ceramic workshop in the Mochlos-Myrsini-Tourloti triangle, with characteristic features very similar to those of the Palaikastro workshop: orange-red fabric, whitish or cream-coloured slip, and red or reddish paint. She also suggested the further investigation of the Tourloti and Mochlos region with the aim of enriching our knowledge about this workshop, see MacGillivray 1997, 206-207.
[45] EAM 14624, 14625, and 14626. These confiscated vases entered the National Archaeological Museum in 1970, see *appendix*.
[46] Mylonas 1972-1973, 38, pl. 24c, 25: a large amphora with traces of the textile in which it was originally wrapped.
[47] See Paschalidis 2007, 434, pl. 107d (right) and Paschalidis 2005, 34-35 for, among other things, the copper-alloy dagger NAM 10811 from Andronianoi,

the LMIIIA2/B chamber tomb at Agios Ioannis, Chania,[48] and the slightly later, Protogeometric tomb at Foinikia, Herakleion.[49] The textile traces on the rim and neck of certain LHIIIA2 vases from the graves at Pylona, Rhodes, were interpreted as remains of what sealed their contents.[50] Finally, the traces of textile remains on the skeletal remains of Chamber Tomb I at Gra Lygia, Ierapetra (LMIIIA2/B) may belong to the deceased's garments or shrouds, or to the sacks in which the bones were placed after their removal.[51] Either way, the unanticipated preservation of such finds enriches our picture of burial customs in the prehistoric Aegean.

The comparative study of the vases from the chamber tomb excavated by Tsipopoulou at Tourloti may shed some light on certain 'political' and cultural characteristics of East Crete in the LMIIIA period. Thus, the piriform jar (SM 4511), which dates to the LMIIIA1 or early LMIIIA2 period and originates from a Knossos workshop, illustrates the wide distribution of the products of Crete's Mycenaean capital shortly before its definitive collapse. These Knossian vases, which represent the local version of the Mycenaean Aegean's pottery styles,[52] were imported into East Crete primarily before, but also after the great palace's end.[53] By contrast, the trefoil-spouted jug (SM 4512), which is contemporary with the piriform jar, comes from a workshop near Tourloti and preserved earlier features of Minoan domestic pottery, such as the dipped decorative style, the paintbrush splashes, the drips, the use of string for the removal of the vase from the wheel, etc. All of these features characterize the conservative types, or type-fossils, in many East Cretan sites.[54] These local types either coexisted quietly with the elaborate decorations of the Creto-Mycenaean repertoire, as is often the case in the LMIIIA funerary assemblages in East Crete,[55] or were the dominant vases of daily life, as suggested for example by certain rooms at Palaikastro, which date from the first reoccupation (LMII and LMIIIA1-2),[56] and the contents of the houses at Mochlos

---

Euboea, with part of the textile that originally covered the entire object.

[48] Karantzali 1986, 75, fig. 17: the grave gifts included a copper-alloy bowl with part of the textile that originally covered it.

[49] Grammatikaki 1998, 239, n. 288: a copper-alloy bowl with traces of the textile in which it was originally wrapped.

[50] De Wild 2001, 114, colour pl. 2, pls. 34 and 51.

[51] Apostolakou 1998, 85, pl. 24a-h.

[52] Betancourt 1985, 163.

[53] See for example, Smith 2005, 188-190, for the various Knossian vases from Mochlos, which belong to the first reoccupation phase (LMII - LMIIIA1), and 198, for the Knossian kylikes and the amphoroid krater and stirrup-jar from Tomb 2 at Mochlos, which date to the LMIIIB period. Also see Tsipopoulou 1997, 219, 220, fig. 18:d (n. 91.144.2: part of a LMIIIB Knossian krater) and 249, fig. 43:a (ANM 1096: a complete LMIIIA2 Knossian feeding bottle from Petras, Siteia). See Betancourt 1985, 163, for the close relations between Knossos and East Crete in the LMIIIA period. The importation of Knossian products in the LMII-LMIIIA1 periods and its abrupt end at the beginning of the LMIIIA2 period was also noted in the tombs at Psari Forada in the Viannos province and interpreted as the result of the fall of Mycenaean Knossos, see Banou and Rethemiotakis 1997, 50-53.

[54] See MacGillivray 1997a, 278, for the development of local ceramic styles at Palaikastro, Gournia, Episkopi in Ierapetra, etc, from the LMIB period to the peculiar, local LMII and the subsequent period of the first re-occupation in the LMIIIA1/2 period. Also see Smith 2005, 189, 192, 199, with bibliography, for the same conservative ceramic types at Mochlos, their introduction from Palaikastro, their local reproduction, the origin of certain shapes in the LMIB ceramic repertoire, and their role in defining the local social identity that developed in East Crete in the LMIII period. Angus Smith sees the local pottery styles and traditions as a strong indicator of regionalism, which emerged as a result of the LM IB destruction of the Neopalatial administrative centers, long before the final destruction of Knossos (Smith 2002, 75).

[55] See for example, Apostolakou 1998, 35, drawing 11, n. 12656 (LMIIIA2), and 54, drawing 35, n. 12688 (LMIIIA2), for examples of vases of traditional Minoan domestic types from the tombs at Gra Lygia in Ierapetra, found together with ceramic shapes in LMIIIA2 and LMIIIB fashions, and with imported Mycenaean shapes (Apostolakou 1998, 84). Also see Kanta 1980, 166, fig. 106:2-3 (LMIIIA), 165-166, fig. 108:2 and 109:2, 4 (LMIIIA), for the same category of 'conservative' local pottery from tombs at Myrsini, and 148, fig. 57:7, 59:1 (LMIIIA2 or early LMIIIB), for vases of the same category from tombs at Episkopi in Ierapetra. The chamber tombs of Mochlos contained large quantities of the same pottery types; see Smith 2005, 190-191, 192, fig. 5, 197, fig. 8, 198.

[56] MacGillivray 1997a, 277, with bibliography; MacGillivray 1997, 193. Based on the continuation and smooth development of these local ceramic traditions from the Neopalatial period to the LMIIIA2 period and on the absence of symbols of the 'Mycenaean *status quo*' (warrior tombs, Linear B documents, kylikes, etc), Sandy MacGillivray suggested that East Crete, from the Ierapetra Isthmus to Palaikastro, was outside the political and administrative sphere of Mycenaean Knossos, see MacGillivray 1997a, 279.

during the later reoccupation (LMIIIA2-B).[57] The coexistence in this tomb and in a closed deposit of these two very different pottery styles of the LMIIIA1 or early LMIIIA2 periods reflects the different aesthetic approaches and tastes that coexisted in the eastern confines of Mycenaean Crete during this period.[58]

---

[57] Smith 2005, 190-191.

[58] A similar coexistence of the same heterogenous ceramic types was noted in the Mochlos settlement and cemetery during the first reoccupation period (LMII-LMIIIA1), raising questions on the origin and customs of the town's new inhabitants: did they simply adopt the new Knossian fashion of banqueting with kylikes and kraters or were they colonists from Knossos, who brought along new customs and vessels? (Smith 2005, 189-190 and 196-197, for the case of Tomb 15 at Mochlos).

THE CHAMBER TOMB EXCAVATED BY NIKOS PAPADAKIS

The limited information regarding Nikos Papadakis' excavation of a chamber tomb comes from a short report in the Chronicles of the *Archaeologikon Deltion*;[59] no excavation diary, plans, or photographs were found. The excavation is mentioned briefly in Metaxia Tsipopoulou's thorough overview of the investigations in the LMIII sites of the Siteia province.[60] The excavator's report in the *Deltion* mentions a tomb with a short dromos and a dry-stone wall, which blocked the entrance. With a diameter of 2.7 m, the circular chamber preserved part of the roof to a height of 1.6 m. The disturbed state of the chamber's interior was interpreted as the result of a possible looting and of the partial collapse of the roof.

The excavation report mentions no burials inside the chamber; we do not know if any bones were found and, if so, in what state. It lists the following finds: three stirrup-jars, one pyxis lid, one biconical clay whorl, one stone conical whorl, and, finally, one cylindrical faience bead with incised decoration. The Siteia Museum entry book, however, lists four stirrup-jars (SM 5071-5074), one lid (SM 5075), the lower part of a stamnos containing burnt human bones (SM 5078), two whorls, and one faience bead (SM 5079-5081), all from the tomb excavated by Papadakis at Plakalona, Tourloti **(pl.1b)**.

SM 5071. Small globular stirrup-jar (FS 173 or 174, **figs. 8-11**). Complete. Part of the bottom missing, funnel-shaped rim partially recomposed. Large chip on the shoulder, smaller chips around the discoid base. Flaking and areas of white concretions all over. Fine, light brown fabric, light brown slip, brownish-black paint that is fugitive in places. Painted loop around the base of the neck and false neck. Handles elliptical in section, monochrome painted with reserved triangles on top. Slight protruberance on the false neck's disc, which is decorated with concentric circles. Combination of wide and narrow bands on the lower body; two more bands on the slightly ring-shaped base. The main decorative motif, a stylized octopus (FM 21), occupies the upper belly and shoulder. The octopus's head is heart-shaped with monochrome eyes inscribed in circles. Two tentacles begin at the head and end in a curved line under the handles. A second pair of tentacles sprouts from the first pair and winds around the vase to the rear, where it ends on the bands. Complementary motifs suggest a seascape: scale pattern forming triangular clusters that hang from the tentacles (FM 42:21-22), an eight-petaled rosette on the shoulder's backside (FM 17:25), and dotted sea anemonies between the spout and the short pair of tentacles (FM 27:34)

Height: 12.3 cm, maximum diameter: 11.6 cm, base diameter: 4.7 cm.

The globular or biconical stirrup-jar with painted octopus appeared in the LMIIIB period throughout Crete, from Chania, where they probably originated,[61] to Itanos on the east coast. Only the globular stirrup-jar survived into the subsequent LMIIIC phase,[62] and by the end of the twelfth century BC these became among the most popular funerary vases throughout the Creto-Mycenaean Aegean, with numerous local productions and varieties of the Octopus Style.

During the early stage of the Octopus Style, early in LMIIIC, the painted composition occupies loosely the entire surface, with single complementary motifs (rosettes, lozenges, tongue motifs, sea anemones, etc) and large empty spaces, without the *horror vacui* effect of the subsequent mature stage (Close Octopus Style). The octopus representations on two sides of the clay chest-shaped vessel from Kastelli, Pediada date to this early stage of the LMIIIC period.[63] Athanasia Kanta dated the Minoan spherical stirrup-jar with octopus representations from Ialysos in Rhodes[64] and Myrsini near Siteia[65] to this early stage. Another

---

[59] Papadakis 1984.
[60] Tsipopoulou 1995, 186.
[61] Tzedakis 1969, 417; Kanta 1980, 252, 254.
[62] Popham 1967, 347. Colin Macdonald distinguished two types of painted octopus on LMIIIB stirrup-jars, one of which survived into the subsequent LMIIIC period (Macdonald 1986, 138).
[63] Phase A of the LMIIIC occupation of the Minoan building on the hilltop of the modern village (early LMIIIC – beginning of middle LMIIIC period), see Rethemiotakis 1997a, 407, 412-415, fig. 11-15 (views 4 and 6), 417.
[64] Kanta 1980, 305, fig. 99:3-4. Also see Karantzali 1998, 66-67, n. 25.
[65] Kanta 1980, 171, 255, fig. 137:2 (ANM 1904). For the LMIII cemetery at Myrsini, Siteia, see Platon 1959a, 372-373; Daux 1960, 819-821; Kanta 1980, 163-173. The shard of a stirrup-jar with octopus decoration from Knossos (Popham 1965, 329, fig. 8, 332, 341, n. 59) also dates to the early stage of the Octopus Style (early LMIIIC period).

spherical stirrup-jar with an octopus and a combination of wide and narrow bands on the belly comes from the settlement at Kastelli, Chania, and dates to the early LMIIIC period.[66] The Tourloti stirrup-jar excavated by Papadakis (SM 5071) also dates to the early phase of the LMIIIC period.

The two stirrup-jars from Tourloti and Myrsini have the same spherical body, low ring base, and well-shaped vertical handles and neck. Although found in neighbouring sites, they obviously came from different workshops, since the Myrsini vase has a finer, better fired fabric and a finer, more carefully executed decoration. On the other hand, the Tourloti jar shows certain peculiar features. Despite the general rule that the octopus's body extends below the lines that define the decorative panel,[67] the Tourloti octopus has a heart-shaped head and a body that is either indistinct or omitted altogether as a result of stylization. The dotted sea anemones between the short tentacles also occur on the Ialysos jar, though more elaborate. The triangular clusters of scale patterns hanging from the tentacles on the Tourloti vase are among the most popular complementary ornaments during this period.[68] The early LMIIIC kylix from Room 24 at Kavousi-Kastro features similar motifs hanging from the rim and framing the central 'Minoan flower', which resembles octopus tentacles and recalls the painted composition of the Tourloti jar.[69]

The Tourloti stirrup-jar (SM 5071) is the product of an East Cretan workshop and dates to the early stage of the Octopus Style, in the early LMIIIC period.

SM 5072. Small spherical, slightly depressed stirrup-jar (FS 174 or 176, **figs. 12-14**). Complete, restored from two fragments. Incomplete neck, recomposed in a way that deforms the jar's general appearance. Small chips and flaking on entire body. Small white organic concretions in places. Fine, light brown fabric, light brown slip, reddish-brown paint, fugitive in places. Five bands of equal width decorate the surface from the shoulder to the slightly concave base. A double wavy line between the bases of the handles defines a decorative panel filled with four rows of U-shaped motifs (FM 45) and a group of parallel arches (FM 43:13) with a dot in the middle, which resembles an eye. The panel depicts a stylized fish with its head, gills, and scales within an uneven 'watery' outline. On the opposite side of the shoulder, fringed triangular clusters of dotted scale motifs (FM 42:21 and FM 70:2) render the rocks of a seascape. Loops outline the slightly raised handles of elliptical section, leaving reserved triangles on the top. A left-spinning spiral decorates the false spout's flat disc. A painted ring marks the base of the neck.

Height: 9.2 cm, maximum diameter: 8.7 cm, base diameter: 3.4 cm.

Like the previous example (SM 5071), this vase from Tourloti belongs to the large group of LM/LHIIIB-C spherical stirrup-jars that were common in Crete, the Dodecanese, and the Greek mainland.[70] Apart from the stirrup-jar with octopus decoration, the remaining vases of this type produced in Crete are decorated with parallel bands of equal size or, more rarely, with a combination of alternating thin-thick bands, which cover the body from the shoulder to the base. The smaller examples, like the stirrup-jar from the Papadakis excavation, probably served as perfume bottles in life and death or were grave gifts for children.[71] This group includes the small stirrup-jar from Kastelli in Chania,[72] Kalochorafitis in the Pediada,[73] Gra Lygia in Ierapetra,[74] and the Minoan example from Grave 11 at Langada in Kos.[75]

The shoulder of the stirrup-jar from Kos features three 'Minoan flowers' (FM 18:32) formed by multiple stems and triangular clusters of U-shaped

---

[66] Hallager and Hallager 2000, 77, 146, pl. 38, n. 80-P 0260.
[67] Kanta 1980, 254.
[68] Compare Mountjoy 1999, 1099, 1100, n. 70, from Langada, Kos (early LMIIIC).
[69] Coulson 1997, 66, fig. 9:7, 69. Octopuses are also painted on other LM IIIC early pottery shapes, such as kylikes and amphoroid kraters, see Popham 1967, 347.
[70] Kanta 1980, 247, for the LMIIIB-C spherical stirrup-jars, and Mountjoy 1999, 1044-1056 (FS 174, 176) for the Rhodian stirrup-jars, which abound in the LHIIIC period. For the same shape on the Greek mainland see Furumark 1941, 33, 612-614 (FS 174, 176) and Mounjoy 1994, 150-151, fig. 180.
[71] Kanta 1980, 247.
[72] Hallager and Hallager 2003, 175, pl. 57, n. 73-P 0527/1095 (LMIIIB2).
[73] Kanta 1980, 108, fig. 42:6 and 9, n. 18470, with a depressed, spherical body (LMIIIB).
[74] Apostolakou 1998, 76-77, drawing 52 (LMIIIB).
[75] Kanta 1980, 303, fig. 100:3-4 and Mountjoy 1999, 1101, 1103, n. 84 (transitional LMIIIB/C or early LMIIIC).

motifs with fringed edges.[76] Particularly popular in LMIIIB and early LMIIIC pottery,[77] this Cretan motif was the base for the fish composition on the shoulder of the stirrup-jar from Tourloti (SM 5072). The painter of the Tourloti jar varied the 'Minoan flower' that decorates the shoulder of stirrup-jars such as the Kos example by turning the multiple stems sideways to form the fish head and by adding a dot for the eye. He used the flower's U-shaped motifs to render the fish scales and replaced the flower's fringed outline by a band on one side and the usual double wavy line that defines the shoulder decoration on LMIII stirrup-jars on the other.[78] Having thus altered a popular motif, the painter of the Tourloti jar (SM 5072) created a cryptic image, which demands one's full attention in order to be understood. By contrast, a quick glance produces instead the image of a dotted scale motif, like those of the 'rocks' on the opposite side, surrounded by parallel arches, and, next to it, a degenerate 'Minoan flower', framed by the typical double wavy line.

Fringed, triangular clusters of scale motifs on either side of the neck complete the composition on the Kos jar. Common in Cretan and Dodecanesian pottery of the late LMIIIB and early LMIIIC periods,[79] this motif was chosen to render the vegetation-covered rocks in the sea. Clusters of scale motifs occur as complementary ornaments on several other figurative vases, though in different formations and with a different symbolism.[80]

In LH/LMIII vase painting, fish and seascapes are usually rendered with clear designs that refer directly to the object depicted.[81] The two identified painters of vases and larnakes with marine motifs, known as the 'Knossos Fish Master' and the 'Petras-Piskokefalo Group Master', who were active in Central and East Crete, the former in the early LMIIIA1/2 period, the latter early in LMIIIC, created free compositions with fish, marine vegetation, waves, and rocks with an obvious bent for realism.[82] By contrast, the painter of the Tourloti jar (SM 5072) created a 'magic image', either as the result of original, spontaneous inspiration or with the optical illusion in mind.

The small stirrup-jar from Tourloti (SM 5072) is the product of a particular craftsman, probably active in East Crete between the mature LMIIIB and the early LMIIIC periods.

SM 5073. Depressed globular stirrup-jar (FS 171, **figs. 15-17**). Complete, restored from many fragments. Small part of the disc recomposed. Chips and flaking on the entire body. White areas

---

[76] For the definition of the 'Minoan flower' see Popham 1965, 327; Popham 1967, 48 fig. 6:5, 49; Kanta 1980, 305.
[77] Compare Tzedakis 1969, 410 pl. 5 (above), 417 (LMIIIB and early LMIIIC), from Chania; Hallager and Hallager 2003, 164, pl. 56, n. 80-P 0762 (LMIIIB1/2), from Castelli, Chania; Nezeri 2006, 19, 22, pl. 2 n. 2296 (LMIIIB), from Armenoi; Mountjoy 2003, 148-149 n. 795 (LMIIIB), from the South House at Knossos; Rethemiotakis 1997, 316, 317:p (LMIIIB/early LMIIIC), from Kastelli, Pediada; Watrous 1992, 69, fig. 44, n. 1155 (LMIIIB), from Kommos; Popham 1965, 327, 328, fig. 7:39-42, 44-46, 339 and pl. 82:d (LMIIIB), from a site in Central or East Crete; Apostolakou 1998, 54-55, drawing 36, n. 12689 (LMIIIB), from Gra Lygia, Ierapetra, but manufactured at Kydonia. For Minoan stirrup-jars with such flowers found outside Crete, see Mountjoy 1999, 1017, 1019, n. 87 (LMIIIB), from Ialysos; Benzi 1992, 304, pl. 58, n. T32/17 (early LMIIIC) from Ialysos; Kanta 1980, 311, fig. 100:5-6 (LMIIIB), from Enkomi.
[78] For the typical double line that defines the shoulder panel on LMIII stirrup-jars, see for example Apostolakou 1998, 36-37, drawing 13, n. 12658 (LMIIIA2), 44, drawing 23, n. 12674 (LMIIIB), 79-80, drawing 57, n. 12725 (LMIIIB), from Gra Lygia, Ierapetra; Mountjoy 1999, 1020-1021, n. 97 (LMIIIB), for a Minoan vase from Rhodes; Benzi 1992, 356, pl. 89 n. T58/2 (LHIIIB), for a Rhodian stirrup-jar with the same Minoan double line.

[79] For this motif, see for example Hallager and Hallager 2000, 117, pl. 53, n. 70-P 0133 (LMIIIB2/C), from Kastelli, Chania; Rethemiotakis 1997, 316, 319, fig. 28:ab (LMIIIB/early LMIIIC), from Kastelli, Pediada; Popham 1965, 327, 328, fig. 7:43, 339, n. 43 (LMIIIB), from a site in Central or East Crete; Coulson 1997, 64, 65 fig. 8:12 (early LMIIIC) from Kavousi-Kastro; Benzi 1992, 91, for the motif in general (FM 42), and 258, pl. 161, n. T17/11 (early LHIIIC) for the motif on a stirrup-jar from Ialysos.
[80] Sakellarakis 1992, 102, n. 225, from the acropolis of Mycenae (LHIIIA), where the dense, fish-scale network may denote water bubbles; Vermeule and Karageorghis 1982, 207, n. V.140, from Enkomi (LHIIIB2), where the fish appears to pass between two rows of dotted scales forming the opening of an underwater cave.
[81] See for example Vermeule and Karageorghis 1982, V.138, V.141 (LHIIIB), from Cyprus, IX.115, IX.117, IX.119, IX.120 (LHIIIB), X.83-X.87, X.95-X.117 (LHIIIB2/early LHIIIC); Sakellarakis 1992, 101-107 (LHIIIA2 – middle LHIIIC), from the Greek mainland.
[82] For the 'Knossos Fish Master', see Morris 1995. For the 'Petras-Piskokefalo Group Master', see Tsipopoulou and Vagnetti 1997, 474-475, 476, pl. CLXXXI-CLXXXV.

of organic concretions on the side of the belly that lay against the chamber floor. Fine, pinkish-brown clay. Light brown slip, brownish-red, glossy paint. Two groups of wide and narrow bands circle the shoulder, below the handles, and the belly. They alternate with two groups of three bands of equal size on the belly and directly above the monochrome painted ring base. Two pairs of stylized 'Mycenaean flowers' (FM 18:135, 18:140) and a metope with dotted lozenges (FM 75:14, 73:b, 73:3) decorate the shoulder. A painted loop decorates the strap handles, which are slightly higher than the false spout's disc, leaving a reserved triangle on the top and a thin reserved line on the back of each. A fine left-spinning spiral covers the disc. Painted rings mark the flaring rim and base of the narrow, cylindrical spout and the base of the false spout.

Height: 13.7 cm, maximum diameter: 15.1 cm, base diameter: 5.7 cm.

Depressed-globular stirrup-jars decorated with groups of wide and narrow bands alternating with groups of two or three equal sized bands are common in Mycenaean pottery, occurring without interruption from LHIIIA2 until the early LHIIIC period.[83] Stirrup-jar SM 5073 from Tourloti belongs to the late examples of this shape on account of its decoration, which is typical of the LH/LMIIIB and early LH/LMIIIC periods. The shoulder decoration combines stylized 'Mycenaean flowers' and a metope with dotted lozenges. The combination of the flower and metope is particularly popular on the Greek mainland and Crete in the LH/LMIIIB period.[84] The particular variant of the flower pictured on the SM 5073 jar from Tourloti, however, is unparalleled in the rest of the Aegean. Unlike the flower, the metope with dotted lozenges occurs on several LHIIIB vases from both the centre, and the periphery of the Mycenaean world.[85]

In Crete, the slightly depressed, somewhat 'heavy' globular body of stirrup-jar SM 5073 (FS 176: voluminous body, short handles, short neck and false spout placed close together, discoid, slightly concave base) appears in the LMIIIC period,[86] and, as argued below, characterizes the Octopus Close Style stirrup-jar of East Crete in particular. A good example of this shape is the Minoan stirrup-jar from Giapyli, Kos, which dates to the early LMIIIC period.[87] Stirrup-jar SM 5073 from Tourloti is almost identical to two stirrup-jars from Ialysos in Rhodes,[88] another from Fanes, Rhodes,[89] and a fourth fragmentary example from Phaistos.[90] All four date to the mature LHIIIB – early LHIIIC periods. They have a slightly depressed spherical shape, with short handles, neck, and false spout, and are decorated with the same combination of groups of thin-thick bands and a group of equal sized bands at the body's maximum diameter. They differ from one another and from jar SM 5073 only in the shoulder decoration. Despite the presence of 'Minoan flowers' on one of the two stirrup-jars from Ialysos, all four examples and the jar from Tourloti can be attributed, if not to the same workshop, at least to the ceramic production of North Rhodes in the LHIIIB and early LHIIIC periods.

---

[83] Furumark 1941, 33, 611-612 (FS 171, FS 173), 613-614 (FS 176); Mountjoy 1999, 123-124, n. 188 (LHIIIA2), from Mycenae, 346, 349, n. 99 (LHIIIB2 – early LHIIIC), from Pylos, 1093, 1094, n. 47 (LHIIIB), from Langada, Kos; Benzi 1975, 333, pl. 31, n. 21 (LHIIIA2-B), from Ligori, Attica; Blegen 1937, 66 note 6, fig. 132, n. 352 (LHIIIA2), from Prosymna; Karantzali 2001, 42, 165, fig. 33, n. 17962 (LHIIIA2), from Pylona, Rhodes; Benzi 1992, 246, pl. 11, n. T10/6 (LHIIIA2), 283, pl. 42, n. T23/6 (LHIIIA2-B), 333, pl. 75, n. T48/5 (LHIIIA2-B), from Ialysos.
[84] Furumark 1941, 294-295, 416-417; Kanta 1980, 251. For examples of the stylized 'Mycenaean flower' on stirrup-jars, see Popham 1984, pl. 182:a (LMIIIC), from the Unexplored Mansion at Knossos; Blegen 1937, fig. 720 n. 67 (LHIIIB1), from Prosymna; Mountjoy 1995, fig. 54, n. 79 (LHIIIB), from the Acropolis; Mountjoy 1999, 674, 675 n. 131 (LHIIIB), from Tanagra, and 1018, 1019, n. 93 (LHIIIB), from Rhodes; Benzi 1992, 243, pl. 7:e, n. T7/5 (LHIIIB), 344, pl. 83:g-h n. T53/9 (LHIIIB), 358, pl. 92:b-c n. T59/10 (LHIIIB), from Ialysos.
[85] See for example Popham 1965, 321, 322, fig. 3:4 (LMIIIB-C), for the same metope with a row of hatched lozenges on a cup from Central or East Crete; Karantzali 2001, 57, 172 fig. 40, 217, pl. 41:c, n. 16773 (middle LHIIIC), from a jug from Pylona, Rhodes; Vagnetti 2000-2001, 108-109, fig. 2, 115 (LHIIIB), for the same metope with a row of dotted lozenges on a pictorial style Italo-Mycenaean krater from Termitito.
[86] As a development of the LMIIIB spherical stirrup-jar, see Kanta 1980, 247, fig. 71:7.
[87] Kanta 1980, 304, fig. 98:1-2.
[88] Mountjoy 1999, 1042, 1053, n. 193 (T17/11); Benzi 1992, 258, pl. 23:e-f, n. T17/11, and 358, pl. 92:b-c, n. T59/10.
[89] Benzi 1992, 412, pl. 129:c.
[90] Borgna 2003, 154, 293, pl. 40:1.2: the author considers the Phaistos vase a product of the Greek mainland.

The Tourloti jar's (SM 5073) careful construction suggests a ceramic workshop that produced distinctive, recognisable products. The shape is flawless, the firing is perfect, and the slip and paint are unusually glossy. The painted decoration shows great precision and a steady hand. For the groups of thin-thick bands, the vase painter had recourse to the 3/3 canon, where two wide bands occupy 2/3 of the total and a group of (always five) finer bands occupies the remaining 1/3. The bands were painted with great care, even the finer ones, which are equally spaced and very rarely merge with one another. The jar's decoration is inspired by the characteristic Mycenaean tendency for schematization and standardization of motifs to such a degree that it is foreign to its contemporary Minoan pottery.

SM 5074. Small perked-up globular stirrup-jar (FS 175 **figs. 18-21**). Complete, restored from four fragments, neck missing and recomposed. Small chips and flaking on the belly. Large, dark area of organic incrustations below the neck to the base, where the jar lay in contact with the chamber's floor. Fine, light pinkish brown fabric. Light brown slip, glossy brownish red paint turned black on one spot on the belly due to uneven firing. Groups of thin-thick bands on the belly and two simple bands above and on the disc of the flat base. The shoulder's large decorative panel begins lower than the base of the handles. It features a large monochrome painted lozenge with a dotted outline, a 'tail', and a reserve double line on its vertical axis, inscribed within a lozenge-shaped frame of short, dense lines. Dense wavy lines resembling the tentacles of a degenerate octopus begin on either side of the neck and continue to the base of the handles (FM 24:4). A loop outlines the handles and the edge of the false spout's flat disc. A fine left-spinning spiral decorates the latter. The handles - of elliptical section - are slightly higher than the false spout's disc.

Height: 11.5 cm, maximum diameter: 10.5 cm, base diameter: 4.1 cm.

The perked-up globular shape (FS 175) of stirrup-jar SM 5074 from Tourloti characterizes many Aegean LH/LMIIIC stirrup-jar.[91] Several examples, particularly of the early LHIIIC period, come from nearby Rhodes.[92] The numerous East Cretan examples are mentioned below in the discussion of the Phygetakis stirrup-jar SM 4028. One of these examples, namely the stirrup-jar from the Petras cemetery, is probably the best parallel for stirrup-jar SM 5074 in terms of shape.[93]

The dense wavy lines on the jar's shoulder suggest the tentacles of an octopus, as they appear on the LMIIIB octopus stirrup-jars from Chania. As mentioned above, many of these stirrup-jars were exported to East Crete.[94] Isolated attempts by Ierapetra workshops to imitate this new decorative style demonstrate an inclination to experimentation with the early Octopus Style.[95] In the subsequent LMIIIC period, this inclination developed into a local 'school' of Octopus Style stirrup-jars, which includes, apart from stirrup-jar SM 5071 from Tourloti mentioned above, a large number of larnakes, such as those of the so-called 'Petras-Piskokefalo Group Master', which feature, among other characteristics, dense wavy lines for octopus tentacles.[96] Thus, the dense wavy lines on either side of the neck of stirrup-jar SM 5074 place the jar's decoration within the artistic production of East Cretan potters of the mature LMIIIB or early LMIIIC.

The shoulder's main decorative motif **(fig. 20)**, however, namely the large monochrome lozenge with dotted outline, the 'tail', and double reserve line on the vertical axis, inscribed in a lozenge-shaped frame of dense lines, is unparalleled in the Aegean; its meaning, if there ever was one, is unknown. Remote parallels can be found in the lozenges decorating the amphorae, jugs, and kylikes of Rhodes.[97] A characteristic motif of the ceramic

---

[91] For Mycenaean stirrup-jars of this shape, see Furumark 1941, 31 fig. 6, 33, 613; Mountjoy 1994, 151 (early LHIIIC), 174-176 (middle LHIIIC), 196 (late LHIIIC). For this shape in Crete, see Kanta 1980, 248.

[92] Benzi 1992, 80 ff; Mountjoy 1999, 1044 ff; the author identifies this shape with type FS 176.

[93] Kanta 1980, 194, fig. 67:9: the author dates the jar to the LMIIIB period. The Petras stirrup-jar, however, may originate from Skyros and probably dates to the end of the LHIIIB or early LHIIIC period (see below the discussion of stirrup-jar SM 4028 from Tourloti).

[94] Kanta 1980, 252-254, particularly fig. 57:1-3; Apostolakou 1998, 57-58, drawing 39.

[95] Kanta 1980, 254, fig. 60:11-12, 69:1-2, 96:4.

[96] Tsipopoulou and Vagnetti 1997, 474-475, 478, pl. CLXXXI-CLXXXVa-b.

[97] These lozenges are either monochrome painted or have a reserve zone along the axis. They usually have a simple line as frame and sometimes a 'tail', see Benzi 1992, pl. 26:f, 29:c, 94:a, 100:c, 108:d; Mountjoy 1999, 1033, 1034, n. 150, 1035, 1036, n. 153, 154, 159, 1064, 1065 n. 248 (early LHIIIC).

workshops of Ialysos,[98] the lozenge may have inspired the peculiar shoulder ornament of the Tourloti stirrup-jar. Another hypothetical interpretation of the motif is that of a sea urchin, which, together with the degenerate octopus tentacles on the other side of the shoulder, may render, in an abstract manner, a seascape.

Unlike the tomb's remaining vases, stirrup-jars SM 5074 and SM 5073 share the same fabric, slip, paint, and excellent firing (**pl. 1b**). Moreover, both are decorated with the groups of thin-thick bands that are characteristic of Mycenaean, rather than Minoan, pottery.[99] The rendering of the bands and of the rest of the decoration, however, is not as careful and precise on stirrup-jar SM 5074 as on SM 5073. Despite these differences both vases can be attributed to the same workshop because of their technical characteristics and common (and exotic for East Crete) decoration of bands. As mentioned above, stirrup-jar SM 5073 may originate from North Rhodes, whereas stirrup-jar SM 5074 may owe its main decorative motif to that same island's ceramic repertoire. Thus, it is possible that these two stirrup-jars were imported into the Tourloti region from North Rhodes in the early LMIIIC period, when East Crete and Rhodes had close relations and the mutual influence in pottery was obvious and very productive.[100]

SM 5075. Cylindrical-discoid lid (FS 334, **figs. 22-25**). Complete, with minor chips and flaking. Areas and spots of dark concretions in and out. Coarse, light brown clay with large black pebble inclusions, thin slip made from the same clay, brown-black paint. Two painted concentric circles and a hole placed off-centre on the disc, another painted circle at the rim.

Height: 2.8 cm, rim diameter: 13.1 cm, disc diameter: 12.6 cm.

Lid SM 5075 was probably used as a cover for ash urn SM 5078. Both objects are made of the same coarse clay, but differ in the colour of the paints, the ash urn having preserved traces of red, not brown-black, paint. A noteworthy feature is that the disc's circles were painted counter-clockwise beginning from the same radius (**fig. 25**).

Lids of this shape are common in the LMII-III pottery,[101] also occur in the Dodecanese,[102] and are rare in the Greek mainland.[103] The simple painted decoration with concentric circles on the disc and another at the rim is characteristic of LMIIIC lids.[104] The Tourloti lid (SM 5075) is dated to this period.

SM 5078. Fragment of a globular stamnos or amphora (FS 64, **figs. 26-27**). Only the flat base and part of the belly to the base of the shoulder is preserved. The surface is chipped and has flaked. Brown fabric with large inclusions of black pebbles. Area on the preserved shoulder base soaked with organic incrustations. Little of the original decoration is preserved: a small area of thin slip from the same clay as the body and traces of two painted red bands placed a little higher than the maximum diameter.

---

[98] Mountjoy 1999, 987.
[99] See the discussion of the Mycenaean stirrup-jar 12690 from Gra Lygia, Ierapetra, in Apostolakou 1998, 55-56, drawing 37.
[100] For the contacts and mutual influence between Crete and Rhodes in this period, see Kanta 1980, 306; Macdonald 1986, 125, 135-138, 149.

[101] See for example Mountjoy 2003, 125, 126, n. 584-585 (LMII), for examples of this shape from the South House at Knossos; Demakopoulou 1997, 110, 111, fig. 19; Popham 1994, 99, pl. 10e; Vermeule and Karageorghis 1982, 74, 209, n. VII.I, for the Knossian figurative lidded pyxis from Chamber Tomb 7 at Mycenae (LMIIIA1); Alexiou 1954 404-409, pl. Z:4, for the famous figurative pyxis with lid from Pachyammos (LMIIIA2). For lids from various sites see Popham 1970, 100 fig. 6:3, pl. 7:c, d, f (LMIIIA1), from the Knossos palace; Hatzaki 2005, 161, 162, n. 257, 258 (LMIIIA1), from the Little Palace at Knossos; Dimopoulou and Rethemiotakis 1978, 65-68, drawing 19, pl. 16 (below), n. IV10/21807 (LMIIIA2), from Metochi Kalou, Herakleion; Bosanquet and Dawkins 1923, 95-97, fig. 79, 80 (LMIIIA2), from Palaikastro; Banou and Rethemiotakis 1997, 40-42, fig. 18:1, 2 (LMIIIA2), from Psari Forada; Hallager and Hallager 2003, 229-230, pl. 66:70-P, 1121 (LMIIIB2), from Chania; Watrous 1992, 100, n. 1720, fig. 64:1720 (LMIIIB2), from Kommos; Borgna 2003, 164, 302, pl. 44:8.2, from Phaistos (LMIIIC). Also see Kanta 1980, 281-283, for LMIII pyxides and their lids in general.
[102] See Morricone 1965-1966, 272, fig. 310, n. 293 and 302, from the cemetery at Langada, Kos (LHIIIC).
[103] Where the cylindrical lid with the concave, instead of flat, top (FS 334) is common, see for example Furumark 1941, 78-79, 642, n. 334; Mountjoy 1994, 160, 201 (respectively early and recent LHIIIC), from Perati.
[104] See for example Borgna 2003, 164, 303-304, pl. 44:8.2, 65:7 (above), n. M1646, from Phaistos (LMIIIC); Seiradaki 1960, 18, fig. 12:6, pl. 7:a, from Karfi (recent LMIIIC); Mook and Coulson 1997, 361-362, fig. 36-37:152, from Kavousi-Kastro (recent LMIIIC or settlement's Phase III); Hallager and Hallager 2000, 155, pl. 44: 80-P 0087, from Chania (LMIIIC).

Preserved height: 13.9 cm, maximum diameter: 20.4 cm, base diameter: 12.4 cm.

The shape of stamnos SM 5078 is common in LMIIIC pottery, in both domestic[105] and funerary contexts, where it was used as an ash urn.[106] It usually features two horizontal handles on the shoulder and is decorated with bands and wavy lines. Stamnos SM 5078 probably had the same decoration.

This is the only known ash urn from Tourloti. It contained the remains of the cemetery's only cremation, namely the burnt bones of a man, 20-25 years old, and one burnt bone of a child, 3-7 years old. The simultaneous cremation of more than one body and the placement of their remains inside the same vase are not unknown in Crete in the twelfth century BC. Two clay pyxides from Tomb 2 at Kritsa contained respectively the remains of an adult, 25-35 years old, and an adolescent, 14-15 years old, and those of a man, 35-40 years old, and a child, 5-7 years old.[107] Multiple cremations were also identified at the North Cemetery of Knossos[108] and (a large number of them) Perati.[109] The simultaneous cremation of two bodies and their burial inside the same vase may indicate that the deceased were relatives. In this case, the twin burials of Tourloti and Kritsa might be identified as those of a parent and child.[110]

The study of the bones by Photini McGeorge, presented in Chapter 3, shows that many of the deceased man's bones and almost all of the child's are missing. Most of the bones were not turned to ash even though the pyre reached a high temperature. The absence of much of the remains of the two bodies is probably due to their selective placement inside the stamnos by their relatives.[111] Unfortunately, because of the absence of an excavation diary or other information, it cannot be excluded that some of the burnt bones were not collected during excavation.

The hypothesis that the custom of incinerating the dead reached the Aegean from Asia Minor, namely from the Hittites, the Mittanni, and Trojans, in the Late Bronze Age is almost unanimously accepted.[112] Most of the cremations in LM Crete are concentrated in a large number of sites in the island's east: Olous (LMIIIA2-B),[113] Kritsa (LMIIIC),[114] Fotoula Praisos (LMIIIC),[115] Myrsini

---

[105] Like the amphora or stamnos from the settlement at Kastelli in Pediada, see Rethemiotakis 1997a, 409, 410, fig. 7; Rethemiotakis 1997, 310 fig. 11c, 311, footnote 11 (early LMIIIC or settlement's Phase A). For a similar amphora from Chalasmenos, Ierapetra, see Tsipopoulou 2005, 322, 325, fig. 22, n. 95-71 (middle LMIIIC), and for the stamnoi from Karfi, see Seiradaki 1960, 6, fig. 3:10, pl. 1:e (recent LMIIIC).

[106] The ash-urns from Pezouloi Atsipades are similar stamnoi or small amphorae, see Petroulakis 1915, 49 fig. 1; also, Agelarakis, Kanta and Moody 2001, 72, fig. 8, 73 fig. 10 (LMIIIC). In mainland Greece similar stamnoi/ash-urns were found at Perati (Iakovidis 1969-1970, vol. B, 32, 40, and vol. C, pl. 166 and 174:19) and Argos (Piteros 2001, 112, fig. 35-36, 113 (middle and recent LHIIIC). It should be noted, however, that the most common ash-urns in East Crete in the LMIIIC period are the cylindrical pyxides, see for example the pyxis from Tomb A at Mouliana (Xanthoudidis 1904, 36, n. 2, pl. 3 below left), the pyxis from Fotoula in Praisos (Platon 1960, 305, pl. 243b, 244a), the pyxides from Kritsa (Tsipopoulou and Little 2001, 85-86, fig. 2-4, 91-92, n. 172-173), and the pyxis from Palaimylos (Davaras 1973, 158-160, with parallels, pl. 28:1-2).

[107] Tsipopoulou and Little 2001, 87-88. The belief – based on the interpretation of cremation as an expression of fear towards the deceased, from which children were exempted as "pure and harmless creatures" (Melas 2001, 22-26) – that children were generally not cremated should, therefore, be reconsidered.

[108] Cavanagh and Mee 1998, 94, footnote 38.

[109] Cavanagh and Mee 1998, 94. Also see Iakovidis 1969-1970, vol. B, 32-36, 38 (plate), 41. The identification of single or multiple cremations requires a special examination of the skeletal remains, which most excavations of tombs with cremations lack, as Spyridon Iakovidis remarks (1969-1970, vol. B, 32, note 1).

[110] Simultaneous burials of mothers with their children are reported, among other areas, from the Mycenaean cemetery at Klauss in Achaea (Papadopoulos 1989, 61; Papadopoulos 1990, 52; Papadopoulos 1992, 56-57). Two mothers were found deposited with their infants and one with a child of 5 - 6 years old, all dated to the middle LH IIIC period, see Paschalidis and McGeorge (forthcoming).

[111] This practice is generally observed in jar burials, see for example Cavanagh and Mee 1998, 94; Iakovidis 1969-1970, vol. B, 39-40, 42, for the cremations at Perati.

[112] Iakovidis 1969-1970 vol. B, 53-55, 56-57; Davaras 1973, 166-167; Melas 1984, 21, 26, 33; Melas 2001, 17; Dickinson 2006, 73. In the case of the western Peloponnese in the twelfth century BC, however, it is possible that cremation was introduced from Italy (Dickinson 2006, 73), a hypothesis previously excluded (Melas 1984, 24).

[113] Kanta 2001.

[114] Tsipopoulou and Little 2001.

[115] Platon 1960, 305.

(LMIIIC),[116] Mouliana (LMIIIC – Sub-Minoan period),[117] and Palaimylos (LMIIIC).[118] This concentration has rightly been interpreted as the result of the frequent passage of merchants, warriors, and travellers journeying from the Mycenaean metropoleis to the Dodecanese, Asia Minor, and Cyprus,[119] with intermediary stops in the safe anchorages of Mirabello Bay, around which most of the above sites are located. The Tourloti cremation, which dates, on the basis of the shape of the stamnos and the other finds, to the early LMIIIC period, belongs within this framework of cultural and ideological exchange. Moreover, it stands as one of the earliest cremations of the 12th century BC in Crete. Finally, the double jar burial of an adult and child, as seen at Tourloti (stamnos SM 5078) and Kritsa (pyxides 172 and 173), and the pits with cremated remains of adults and children, as seen at Perati,[120] are common in earlier and later cremations in Asia Minor,[121] Syria,[122] and Palestine,[122] suggesting that the custom may originate from those regions.

The finds from the grave excavated by Papadakis cannot be characterized as rich or as grave gifts indicative of the deceased's high social rank. Cremation itself, however, was a costly and time-consuming funerary practice, which required large quantities of timber[123] and a special site for the ritual,[124] and produced a spectacle both impressive and touching.[125] It is possible, therefore, that stamnos SM 5078 from Tourloti contained the remains of a man and child – possibly his child – who died together and who were esteemed and, possibly, distinguished during their lifetime.[126] None of the grave gifts can be securely attributed to this burial because of the lack of excavation records. Moreover, because the excavator could not exclude the possibility of previous looting,[127] it remains unknown whether the cremated bodies were originally accompanied by precious objects now lost. We might tentatively associate with them the stirrup-jar with octopus and the 'magic picture', if these do not belong to a slightly earlier burial of the early LMIIIC period, the whorls, and the faience bead, which may have accompanied the deceased as jewellery or a talisman, as mentioned below. Such minor objects, which often elude the grave robbers' attention, were found in association with several other twelfth-century BC cremations in the Aegean.[128]

SM 5079. Biconical spindle whorl of reddish-brown jasper **(pl. 4c right and fig. 28 left)**. White concretions in places. Small part of the body missing from the centre (maximum diameter) to the flat rim of the hole. Hole circular in section.

Height: 1.9 cm, maximum diameter: 2.2 cm, rim diameter: 0.4 cm.

The stone spindle whorl SM 5079, mentioned as clay by the excavator in his short report,[129] belongs to Iakovidis's first type.[130]

SM 5080. Conical spindle whorl of black steatite with greyish-white veining **(pl. 4c left and fig. 28 right)**. Part of the top missing.

---

[116] Platon 1960, 305, where the cremation at Myrsini, Siteia, is referred to as "known" and is dated to the "end of the LMIIIC period". The only published excavation report for the LMIII cemetery of Myrsini (Platon 1959a, 372-373), however, mentions no such cremation. Information on the LMIIIC cremation from Myrsini is given by Davaras 1973, 162 and n. 48.
[117] Xanthoudidis 1904, 25-26. For the dating of the krater containing a cremation from Mouliana, see Davaras 1973, 163, footnote 56.
[118] Davaras 1973, 158-160, pl. 28:1-2.
[119] Iakovidis 1969-1970, vol. B, 56-57; Melas 1984, 33; Cavanagh and Mee 1998, 97; Kanta 2001, 63, 64-65; Tsipopoulou and Little 2001, 93 (footnote 31), 94; Piteros 2001, 116-117; Tsipopoulou 2005, 328; Thomatos 2006, 177.
[120] Iakovidis 1969-1970, vol. B, 32 (Tomb 1, Pit 2), 34 (Tomb 122, pit).
[121] Iakovidis 1969-1970, vol. B, 54; Melas 1984, 28, for the cemeteries at Osmankaya and Baglarbasikaya (sixteenth – thirteenth centuries BC).
[122] Iakovidis 1969-1970, vol. B, 52, for the cemetery at Hama on the Orontes (end of fifteenth – twelfth centuries BC), and 52-53, for the cemetery at Hazor in southern Palestine (eleventh century BC).
[123] Thomatos 2006, 177.

[124] Iakovidis 1969-1970, vol. B, 41-42.
[125] Dickinson 2006, 181.
[126] Either way, such an impressive ceremony required the acceptance and undertaking of the local authorities, it would have been, in other words, an authorized public funerary practice. The deceased's relatives or others attending the ceremony would have participated in gathering the remains and placing them inside an urn, see Dickinson 2006, 180-181; Thomatos 2006, 177.
[127] Papadakis 1984, 306.
[128] Spedifically faience whorls and beads, see Cavanagh and Mee 1998, 94. For example, four whorls were found inside the pyre in the LHIIIC cemetery at Kamini, Naxos, see Vlachopoulos 2006, 321.
[129] Papadakis 1984, 306.
[130] Iakovidis 1977, 113, 114, fig. 1:1.

Height: 1.3 cm, maximum diameter: 2.1 cm.

Flat-topped conical stone spindle whorl SM 5080 belongs to Iakovidis's third type.[131]

Clay and stone whorls are the most common finds in domestic and funerary LH/LMIII contexts.[132] Usually, one or two whorls accompany each deceased, though burials with more than two or no whorls also exist.[133] Biconical whorls are less common than conical ones though by no means rare.[134]

Despite the scholarly interest generated by these objects, their use in the Creto-Mycenaean Aegean remains an open question: necklace beads, spindle whorls, or buttons.[135] The discovery of eleven stone conical whorls around the ankles of a deceased woman in Tomb 16 at Perati and a similar discovery in Tomb 19 at Nauplion led to the hypothesis that the whorls might have been sewn onto the garment's hem as weights in order to create folds.[136] Several groups of whorls from female burials have been interpreted accordingly in recent years,[137] even though the number of objects did not always suffice for such a use. Single or pairs of whorls have also been identified as ornaments or weights attached to the belts of garments on the basis of iconographic parallels.[138] Finally, a recent study by the Centre for Textile Research at Copenhagen demonstrated that the common Creto-Mycenaean whorls were ideal for spinning wool.[139]

One can only hypothesize on the use of the two whorls (SM 5079 and SM 5080) from the tomb excavated by Papadakis. If they accompanied the cremated remains of the man and child in stamnos SM 5078, they were probably not spinning implements. Moreover, their limited number makes their use in jewellery or as garment weights improbable. Eleni Konstantinidi suggests a more plausible interpretation for these objects, which are often found alone or in pairs, as mentioned above. She proposes that they were used to secure the shroud or other textile in which the cremation remains were wrapped.[140]

SM 5081. Cylindrical faience bead (**pl. 4c middle and fig. 29**). Shiny, light blue surface. Two incised lines below the upper and lower edge with dense hatching in between.[141]

Height: 0.9 cm, diameter: 0.8 cm.

Faience bead SM 5081 belongs to a type common in the Mycenaean world, namely the 'tubular bead with incised decoration' (according to Agnes Xenaki-Sakellariou)[142] or *Gitternetzzylinderperlen*

---

[131] Iakovidis 1977, 113, 114, fig. 1:3.
[132] Iakovidis 1977, 113, 116. For LMIII whorls see for example Hallager 2000, pl. 96, 99, 105c, 113a, 113d and Hallager 2003, 266-267, pl. 148, 149, from Kastelli, Chania (respectively from LMIIIC and LMIIIB2 levels); Popham 1984, 239, pl. 218:7, 219:5, 232:25, from the Unexplored Mansion at Knossos (LMIIIA-B); Sakellarakis and Sakellaraki 1997, 584 and fig. 597, from Tholos Tomb A (LMIIIA1) and the Mycenaean burial enclosure at Archanes (LMIIIA); Papadopoulou 1997, 324, 337, fig. 26, 338, from the tholos tomb at Armenoi, Rethymno (LMIIIA); Karantzali 1986, 76, 77 fig. 18:T1-T3, from the chamber tomb at Agios Ioannis, Chania (LMIIIB).
[133] Iakovidis 1977, 116-117 and Iakovidis 1969-1970, vol. B, 278, for the Perati cemetery.
[134] At Perati, the analogy between conical and biconical whorls is 114:1 (Iakovidis 1969-1970, vol. B, 280) and at Pylona, Rhodes, 3:2 (Karantzali 2001, 76, 77, pl. 50:b).
[135] For the history of the question, see Iakovidis 1969-1970, vol. B, 279; Iakovidis 1977, 114 ff; Vlachopoulos 2006, 320-323, with bibliography. Doniert Evely regarded the LMIIIA-B whorls from the Unexplored Mansion at Knossos as buttons for garments, see Popham 1984, 239.
[136] Iakovidis 1977, 117-118; Iakovidis 1969-1970, vol. B, 60, fig. 4, 279, and vol. C, pl. 73:d, 74:b.
[137] Sakellarakis and Sakellaraki 1997, 584, for the whorls from Tholos Tomb A and the Mycenaean burial enclosure at Archanes; Karantzali 2001, 76, for the whorls from the cemetery at Pylona, Rhodes.
[138] Iakovidis 1977, 118 (and footnote 59), 119.
[139] On the basis of experiments that used remarkably exact copies of Creto-Mycenaean whorls, see Andersson (forthcoming). Elisabeth Barber (1991, 51-68) describes in detail the shapes and uses of whorls in the Eastern Mediterranean and the Near East in the third – second millennia BC.
[140] Konstantinidi, 2001, 235, for a long discussion of the possible use of whorls in both male and female burials. Athanasia Kanta makes the same hypothesis for the three whorls accompanying the 'warrior-landowner' in the LMIIIB tomb at Agios Ioannis, Chania, see Kanta 2003, 179. Traces of textiles on the bones inside a LMIIIA2/B tomb at Gra Lygia, Ierapetra, were interpreted as the remains of sacs in which the bones were placed after the body's decay, see Apostolakou 1998, 85-86.
[141] Maria Effinger (Effinger 1996, 306) also mentions bead SM 5081 as "cylindrical with incised decoration, of faience".
[142] Xenaki-Skellariou 1985, 295, n. 28.

(according to Georg Nightingale),[143] which dates to the LHIIIA to LHIIIC periods. This type was also popular in Palestine and Cyprus, where it appeared in the Late Cypriot II period[144] and where it might originate from – unless, as suggested by Nightingale, the type is a Mycenaean invention exported into the Eastern Mediterranean.[145]

In the Aegean, the greatest concentration of this type of faience bead was found in the chamber tombs of Mycenae, where each tomb contained two or more beads (total of 25 beads).[146] Thirteen beads of this type were found in Room 19 of the Temple Complex in Mycenae's Religious Centre as part of the so-called 'cache of small objects'.[147] Tomb III at Englianos[148] and the pit graves at Kokolata in Kefallonia[149] each contained four identical beads of this type; the Tiryns hoard[150] and the tombs of Elateia in Fthiotis[151] each contained three. Two such beads come from Ialysos[152] and single examples from the tombs at Dendra,[153] Katarraktis[154] and Klaus[155] in Achaea, and Pylona in Rhodes.[156]

The relative abundance of these ornaments at Mycenae compared to the rest of the Mycenaean world and their presence in the three most important Mycenaean centres, namely, Mycenae, Tiryns, and Pylos, suggest a centralized production and distribution. Although a workshop specializing in the production of Mycenaean faience has not yet been identified,[157] it is most likely that the production of faience was exclusive to the palaces, as was that of glass.[158] The distribution mechanism for luxury goods was probably well organized since it supplied the markets from central Greece and the Ionian to Crete and the Dodecanese.[159] Most of the examples mentioned above belong to the this period: the beads of Mycenae (LMIIIA-IIIB), possibly those of the Tiryns hoard,[160] those of Pylos (LMIIIA-IIIB), Dendra (LMIIIA), Elateia (LMIIIA-IIIC), Pylona (LMIIIA2), and most probably the large group of faience beads from the Mavroeidis excavations at Tourloti (**fig. 1**),[161] which does not, however, include this particular type of bead.

After the fall of the palaces at the end of the LHIIIB period and throughout the LHIIIC period, faience jewellery remained in use, often in abundance, as in the rich Perati cemetery.[162] Because, however, of the general decline in quality and quantity of jewellery during this period,[163] of the old Mycenaean repertoire only the simplest shapes, such as the cylindrical bead with hatched decoration, survived.[164] Several beads belong to this later period: the examples from Ialysos, Katarraktis,

---

[143] Nightingale 2004, 171, 172, fig. 1:9.
[144] Benzi 1992, 197; Karantzali 2001, 75.
[145] Nightingale 2003, 313; Nightingale 2007, 425.
[146] Xenaki-Sakellariou 1985, 295 n. 28.
[147] Moore and Taylour 1999, 13-20, particularly fig. 5, n. 68-1525, pl. 6 (LHIIIB2). The cache's small finds (a comb, figurines, plaques, beads, a scarab, of bone, rock-crystal, amber, glass, steatite, and faience), found inside a clay cup in Room 19, were interpreted as offerings to the temple (Moore and Taylour 1999, 80).
[148] Blegen et al. 1973, 90, fig. 172:14 (Tholos Tomb III).
[149] Four such beads were found in the pit graves at Kangelisses, Kokkolata, which date, on the basis of unpublished pottery finds, to the LHIIIA2-IIIC periods, see Kavvadias 1912, 263 fig. 41:b, 265 fig. 44:a and Souyoudzoglou-Haywood 1999, 59, 84.
[150] Spyropoulos 1972, 183, pl. 27a, 29.
[151] The dating of the beads from Elateia will be given in the final publication of the Greek-Austrian excavation. For the preliminary study and presentation of the glass and faience beads from the cemetery, see Nightingale 2003.
[152] Benzi 1992, 197, pl. 121. The first bead comes from Tomb 53/A4, the second from Tomb 71/A.
[153] Persson 1931, 30, n. 23, pl. 15.
[154] Papadopoulos 1978-1979, 142, 223, n. 20 (PMX.5), fig. 290b and 325:6.
[155] Unpublished. Found with the burial of a woman, 12-20 years old, in Tomb *Theta*. With it were four more carnelian beads, a copper-alloy tool, and a late LHIIIC (or Phase 5) stirrup-jar. For the Mycenaean cemetery at Klaus, Patras, see Paschalidis and McGeorge (forthcoming).
[156] Karantzali 2001, 75, 174, fig. 42:567e, pl. 50c.

[157] Panagiotaki 2002, 38.
[158] Triantafyllidis 2002-2005, 176-177, with footnotes, for the palatial glass workshops at Mycenae, Tiryns, Thebes, Athens, Midea, and Pylos.
[159] Nightingale 2003, 313.
[160] The dating of the three cylindrical beads with incised decoration from the Tiryns Hoard is part of the great discussion on the hoard's character and origin. Joseph Maran's hypothesis (Maran 2006, 130-131, 141), however, that the hoard comprises the heirlooms of one of the ruling families of Tiryns suggests a palatial (LHIIIA-B) date for the three beads and their first use by members of the palatial elite.
[161] Mavroeidis 1938, 219. Also see introduction, above.
[162] Where 103 faience beads were found, see Iakovidis 1969-1970, 303 ff. The LMIII cemetery at Tourloti also yielded two fragmentary bow fibulae with unusual decoration of small cylindrical faience beads passed through the bow, which were found inside a LMIIIC clay tub larnax, see Tsipopoulou and Vagnetti 1999, 136-138, fig. 9:d-e.
[163] Konstantinidi 2001, 212.
[164] Nightingale 2007, 427, footnote 43; Nightingale 2003, 313.

Klaus, possibly those from Kokollata, and bead SM 5081 from Tourloti, the only example of this type found so far in Crete.[165]

Most of these beads were unique examples, unlike the earlier finds from Mycenae, Tiryns, and Pylos, which were probably parts of necklaces. Single examples from Cyprus and Ialysos were interpreted as having belonged to earrings, because of their position near the deceased's body.[166] It appears, however, that in the Mycenaean world, single beads of glass or carnelian often accompanied children's burials.[167] It has also been suggested that faience ornaments symbolized the hope for rebirth or the deceased's immortality, hence their popularity as grave gifts with talismanic properties.[168]

If bead SM 5081 does not belong to another burial, which was lost or went unrecorded by the excavator, it might be interpreted as either part of the earring worn by the man buried inside stamnos SM 5078 or as an ornament or talisman belonging to the child.

---

[165] The cylindrical bead with incised cross-hatched decoration is not included in Effinger's exhaustive study on Minoan jewellery (1996), nor is it known from more recently published contexts.
[166] Benzi 1992, 197, note 26.
[167] Konstantinidi 2001, 244, who also mentions that the spherical or amygdaloid carnelian beads might have indicated the child's sex.
[168] Panagiotaki 2002, 52-53, and Panagiotaki 2000, 159, 160, in the discussion on faience jewellery production in Egypt and Minoan Crete.

THE VASES PRESENTED BY MANOLIS FYGETAKIS

Of the seven vases handed in by Manolis Fygetakis and kept in the storerooms of the Siteia Archaeological Museum (Siteia Museum inventory numbers 4023-4029; previous Agios Nikolaos Museum inventory numbers 4561 – 4567), only six are presented here (pl. 2a), since it was impossible to locate the seventh, namely small fragmentary jug SM 4029. The Octopus Style stirrup-jar SM 4026 (pls. 4a, 4b and figs. 48-53) is presented in this volume's second part together with a discussion on its identification as the work of a specific East Cretan potter, conventionally dubbed the 'Xanthoudidis Master'.

SM 4023 (ANM 4561). Globular jug (FS 109, **figs. 30-31**). Almost complete. Cracks on the neck and the lower body, small part of the belly missing. Flaking around the discoid base. Concretions in places. Fine, yellowish-brown fabric, same slip, brown paint, turned red and fugitive in places. Uneven firing. Painted ring on the simple, flaring rim, another on the base of the neck and handle. Painted ring around the disk of the slightly concave base. Handle circular in section. Two bands of equal width at the belly's maximum diameter. Drip of paint on the belly above the bands; smaller drip below the base of the handle.

Height: 16.6 cm, maximum diameter: 14 cm, base diameter: 7 cm.

Globular-ovoid jugs with a wide, concave neck (small: FS 112-115, medium: FS 109-110, large: FS 105-107), decorated with bands on the rim, base of neck, maximum diameter, and base, are a common and characteristic shape of LMIIIA2-C pottery with a wide distribution.[169] Examples are known from Achaea,[170] Vourvatsi in Attica,[171] Prosymna,[172] the houses of the North Slope of the Athenian Acropolis,[173] the Mitsotakis Collection (possibly from the Peloponnese),[174] Langada in Kos,[175] Ialysos,[176] and many other locations. In Crete, the same shape, but undecorated, dates from the LMIIIA period onwards.[177] The decorated version, with plain bands or bands of simple motifs on the shoulder, appears in the LMIIIB and IIIC periods[178] in the cemeteries of Episkopi in Ierapetra,[179] Gra Lygia in Ierapetra,[180] Armenoi,[181] the settlement of Agia Aikaterini (Kastelli) in Chania,[182] the chamber tombs of Chania,[183] the excavations for the extension of the Knossos Stratigraphical Museum,[184] Karfi,[185] and elsewhere. Jug SM 4023 from Tourloti closely resembles the Knossos examples in size, form, and band arrangement, and can therefore be dated to the early LMIIIC period.

SM 4024 (ANM 4562). Small beak-spouted jug (FS 149, **figs. 32-33**). Complete, slightly chipped on the edge of the spout and on the plain, flaring rim. Area of organic incrustations on the back of the handle. Yellowish-brown fabric, with few organic inclusions. Black, fugitive paint. Cylindrical neck, handle ovoid in section, depressed globular body, slightly concave, diskoid base. Painted band with drip inside the rim. Outside of rim and neck probably monochrome painted. Reserve band on maximum diameter and wide painted band lower on the belly. Large band covers the base disk with monochrome painted underside.

---

[169] Furumark 1941, 34, 104, who claims that the shape originates with MH jugs, which imitated metal prototypes. Also see Mountjoy 1994, 106-107, fig. 120, 121 (LHIIIB1), 148-149, fig. 175-176 (early LHIIIC), 192-193, fig. 240, 241 (late LHIIIC).
[170] Papadopoulos 1978-1979, 93, 209, fig. 153e, n. PM 431 (LHIIIA2).
[171] Benzi 1975, 312-313, pl. 27 n. 464 (LHIIIB).
[172] Shelton 1996, 15, Tomb 6, n. 31 (NAM 6827), 330, drawing 8 (LHIIIB1/2).
[173] Mountjoy 1995, 45-46, fig. 59:4, n. AP219 (early LHIIIC).
[174] Tsipopoulou 1992, 278, n. 346 (early LHIIIC).
[175] Morricone 1965-1966, 102, 109 fig. 88 n. 282, 165-166 fig. 170 n. 122, 203 fig. 214 n. 161, 302-303 (LHIIIC).
[176] Benzi 1992, 50, 248, pl. 13c, n. T12/7 (early LHIIIC), 259, pl. 25b, n. T17/20 (early LHIIIC), 303, 311, pl. 57e-g, n. T32/7, 8, d (early LHIIIC), 331, pl. 74a, n. T47/1 (LHIIIC early), 384, pl. 104h, n. T75/1 (LHIIIB), 398, pl. 112i, n. T87/9 (early LHIIIC).
[177] See for example Warren 1997, 167 fig. 19 (below right), 169, n. P673 (LMIIIA2), from the Stratigraphical Museum excavations at Knossos.
[178] Kanta 1980, 261-262, note 1. Peter Warren and Eleni Hatzaki note the appearance of this type of jug at Knossos in the early LMIIIC period (Warren 1997, 182; Hatzaki 2007, 249-250).
[179] Kanta 1980, 150, fig. 57:5 and 57:8 (LMIIIB).
[180] Apostolakou 1998, 31, drawing 5, n. ANM 12650 (LMIIIB).
[181] Protopapadaki 1999, 241 n. 221 (LMIIIB).
[182] Hallager and Hallager 2000, 34, 150, pl. 41, 57a, n. 71- P 0880 (LMIIIB2/C).
[183] Matz 1951, 72, 74, pl. 56 n. 725 (LMIIIB).
[184] Hatzaki 2007, 249-250, fig. 6.37:5 (LMIIIC early).
[185] Seiradaki 1960, 14, 15, fig. 9, Type 7, pl. 5a, d (late LMIIIC).

Height: 8 cm, maximum diameter: 6.5 cm, base diameter: 3 cm.

Jug SM 4024 from Tourloti is a miniature version of the ovoid-globular beak-spouted jug, which appeared in Minoan pottery in the EMI period and was produced in all of the pottery styles for almost two millennia.[186] The piriform-ovoid beak-spouted jar was adopted by the Mycenaean repertoire in the LHIIA period[187] and knew several variations in shape and decoration until the beginning of the LH/LMIIIB period,[188] when it was replaced throughout the Aegean by the wide-necked globular-ovoid jug, such as jug SM 4023 from Tourloti examined above.

Jug SM 4024 from the Fygetakis submission imitates the shape of the piriform-ovoid beak-spouted jugs of the LMIIIA period, known in East Crete from the tombs at Myrsini[189] and Gra Lygia in Ierapetra.[190] Miniature beak-spouted jugs are the most common grave gifts in tombs of the LMIIIA and LMIIIB periods[191] and can therefore be interpreted as vases necessary in funerary rituals. One of the earliest miniature vases of this type was found in the Artsa chamber tomb in Pediada, Herakleion.[192] The largest group of Minoan miniature beak-spouted jugs comes from two graves at Kalochorafitis in the Mesara.[193] The miniature beak-spouted jug from the cremation cemetery at Pezouloi Atsipadon in Rethymno, one of the latest examples of this type of grave gift, dates to the middle-late LMIIIC – Sub-Minoan period.[194]

In East Crete, similar vases have been found in the tombs at Gra Lygia[195] and Episkopi,[196] Ierapetra. However, the miniature beak-spouted jug from Tourloti is identical to the beak-spouted jug HM 17086 from the chamber tomb at Adromyloi in Siteia. This vase, which, like the Tourloti example, features plain bands on the body, dates to the LMIIIB period.[197] The similarity between these two vases and proximity of their find spots suggest that jug SM 4024 from Tourloti also dates to the LMIIIB period and that both jugs were made in the same workshop located somewhere in the wider Siteia region.

SM 4025 (ANM 4563). Lightly depressed globular stirrup-jar (FS 176, **figs. 34-36**). Part of the flat disc, one handle, part of the lower belly, and base missing. Chips on the rim, handle, and most of the surface. Fine, pinkish-brown fabric. Thick, yellowish-brown slip. Brown, fugitive paint. The attachment of the false spout, which was made separately, on the jar's shoulder is visible on the interior. Traces of a spiral or concentric circles on the disc's small, central tip. Monochrome painted bands circle the flaring rim and base of the neck, which is decorated with two horizontal lines. On the preserved handle's base is a horizontal line, from which begin three vertical lines, two on the edges and one in between. A pair of straight and another of wavy vertical lines begin below the handle. Of the ornate octopus composition (FM 21), which originally covered much of the jar's upper half, only two areas are preserved: below the neck, where the octopus's head is visible, and on the reverse, where one of the tentacles ends. On the first area, a monochrome painted disc surrounded by concentric circles denotes the eye. Slightly higher, on the forehead, is a monochrome painted 'egg', on either side of which sprout two peculiar hatched 'antennae'. A partially preserved pair of tentacles sprouts from between the eyes and antennae, like a tongue-shaped ornament (FM 19).

---

[186] See for example, Betancourt 1985, pl. 2F (EM I), pl. 4A (EM IIB), pl. 5B (EM III), pl. 6D (MM I), pl. 10E, pl. 11D (MMIIB), pl. 15D (LMI), pl. 21A, pl. 22B, pl. 23E (LMIB), pl. 28E-F (LMIIIA2).
[187] Furumark 1941, 28, 32, 84; Mountjoy 1994, 21.
[188] Furumark 1941, 607, FS 143-145, FS 148. For the shape and its development in Mycenaean pottery, see Mountjoy 1994, 34, fig. 27:1 (LHIIA), 64, fig. 67:1 (LHIIIA1), 81, fig. 88:1-2 (LHIIIA2). For the miniature version of the beak-spouted jug in the Mycenaean ceramic repertoire, see Furumark 1941, 607-608 (FS 149).
[189] Kanta 1980, 165, fig. 67:2, n. ANM 1902, fig. 108:1, n. ANM 1885, fig. 109:1, n. ANM 1875, fig. 110:4, n. ANM 1886 (all LMIIIA1).
[190] Apostolakou 1998, 48-49, drawing 30, n. ANM 12683 (LMIIIA2).
[191] Kanta 1980, 262; Dimopoulou and Rethemiotakis 1978, 57-58.
[192] Xanthoudidis 1904, 19; Kanta 1980, 45, fig. 20:5 n. HM 2572 (LMIIIA2).
[193] Kanta 1980, 109-110, first type of miniature jug (beak-spouted), fig. 127:1-6 (LMIIIA2-B).

[194] Petroulakis 1915, 49 fig. 2 (above, third from left); Kanta 1980, fig. 99:1. For the cemetery at Paizouloi Atsipadon and its recent investigation, see Aggelarakis, Kanta, and Moody 2001.
[195] Apostolakou 1998, 54, drawing 35 n. ANM 12688 (LMIIIA2).
[196] Kanta 1980, 147, fig. 59:6, n. HM 5374 (LMIIIA-B).
[197] Kanta 1980, 185, fig. 72:9, n. HM 17086, where traces of the band decoration are visible.

Consecutive arches, U-shaped motifs (FM 45) in an arched arrangement, and a four-petalled flower, or 'sea anemone' (FM 26:47) complete the composition. The area on the backside shows either the spiralling tip of a tentacle or another octopus's head with monochrome painted eyes inscribed in concentric circles.

Preserved height: 14.8 cm, maximum diameter: 18.9 cm.

Stirrup-jar SM 4025 from Tourloti is a typical example of the Minoan Octopus Close Style[198], or the Close Octopus Style, the term preferred here. The somewhat 'heavy', globular shape (voluminous body, short handles, short neck and false spout placed closely together, discoid base) is characteristic of most stirrup-jars of the LMIIIC period,[199] and, more particularly, as will be discussed below, of the Close Octopus Style stirrup-jar from East Crete.

Despite the decoration's patchy preservation, it is possible to make out the octopus' spiralling tentacles, which consist of complementary concentric semi-circles, some topped with fringes, others with rows of U-shaped motifs, as was common in compositions of this style. The monochrome painted 'egg' on the octopus' forehead occurs frequently on the octopuses of East Cretan workshops, particularly those of the Siteia area, such as the octopus on a plastic rhyton from Tomb 13 at Mochlos[200] and of course the tub larnakes and the stirrup-jars of the 'Petras-Piskokefalo Group Master' **(fig. 67 and pl. 4d right)**, which date to the early LMIIIC period.[201]

The complementary 'sea anemones' is another common motif of the Octopus Style, as seen on two stirrup-jars from Kritsa[202] and Mouliana,[203] and the Cretan stirrup-jar from Tomb B at Aplomata in Naxos.[204]

Another Close Octopus Style, or 'Fringed Style' stirrup-jar from Tourloti, excavated by Richard B. Seager in 1900, is now kept in the Pennsylvania University Museum.[205] Obviously, the two jars came from different workshops. The Seager jar probably comes from a local workshop, less skilled in the art of vase painting. By contrast, the rendering of the composition on jar SM 4025 is tasteful and delicate, almost miniaturistic, as illustrated by the hatched antennae on the octopus' head. The painter used at least two different paintbrushes, a rather inaccurate, wide brush for the bands around the neck and the lines on the handle, and a very fine, steady brush for the marine composition and the almost miniaturistic ornaments, such as those on the preserved area below the neck. The painter of jar SM 4025 recalls the painter of jar SM 4026, or the 'Xanthoudidis Master', whom we will discuss at length below. Both artists show a preference for thin-thick decoration and a steadiness in the use of the fine paintbrush, they render their decorative subject (octopus) with clarity, and give their vases the same spherical form (FS 176).[206]

Octopus stirrup-jar SM 4025 dates to the LMIIIC period, possibly to its middle stages, as already suggested for the mature Close Style of East Crete.[207]

---

[198] For the term's origin, see Kardara 1977, 9. For the Close Octopus Style stirrup-jars, see Kanta 1980, 255-256; Macdonald 1986, 136, 138. For the emergence and development of the Octopus Style in the Aegean and mainland Greece, see Vlachopoulos 1995, 250-251. For a detailed discussion of the Octopus Style in Naxos, see Vlachopoulos 2006, 150 ff. For the characteristics of the Rhodian Octopus Style stirrup-jars, see Macdonald 1985, 212 ff.
[199] Kanta 1980, 247, fig. 71:7.
[200] Nicgorski 1999, 540, pl. CXVI. The Mochlos rhyton probably dates to the LMIIIB period.
[201] Three of the group's four larnakes come from Petras, Piskokefalo, and Agios Georgios Tourtouloi in Siteia. The fourth larnax, of unknown provenance, is now in the Musée d'Art et d'Histoire in Geneva. The Octopus Style stirrup-jar from Tomb 15/2 at Ialysos was attributed to the same potter (Tsipopoulou and Vagnetti 1997, 474-475, 476, pl. CLXXXI-CLXXXV).

[202] ANM 180, see Kanta 1980, 255, fig. 136:1.
[203] HM 3481, see Kanta 1980, 255, fig. 82:8-9, 121:3; Xanthoudis 1904, pl. 1 (below).
[204] NM 914, see Kardara 1977, 18-19, drawing 8, pl. 20, 21a, 36b; Vlachopoulos 2006, 337, 338 fig. 93, pl. 106, colour pl. 7 (below).
[205] Betancourt 1983, 52, fig. 14, pl. 12 (n. 137).
[206] It is generally believed that potters and vase painters were the same person in the Aegean of the Late Bronze Age, see Vlachopoulos 2006, 161, 162, for LHIIIC Naxos. Thus, the preference for certain shapes might help distinguish 'schools' or even local ceramic workshops.
[207] For the dating of Minoan stirrup-jars of the Close Octopus Style, see Kanta 1980, 256; Betancourt 1985, 182. Following Kanta's suggestion that the Close Style was imported at Kritsa in a relatively early phase of the LMIIIC period (Kanta 1980, 134-139), Tsipopoulou proposed to date the early Close Style in East Crete to the early LMIIIC period and the mature Close Style to

SM 4027 (ANM 4565). Squat-biconical stirrup-jar (FS 178, **figs. 37-39**). Complete. Handles recomposed with plaster. Small chips on the plain, flaring rim and on the perimeter of the ring base. Very chipped, particularly the upper half. Badly fired. Fine, orange-red fabric, white slip, fugitive, brownish-black paint. Barely visible concentric circles without the central 'eye' on the false spout's flat disc. Rim monochrome painted in and out to the middle of the neck. Loop around the base of the neck, false spout, and handles. Two hatched loops and a hatched triangle (FM 63:8 and FM 61A: 7) decorate the shoulder's semi-circle; similar, hatched decoration, now hardly visible, on the quarter-circles. Densely spaced, horizontal bands of equal width cover the rest of the body down to the ring base. A row of monochrome painted discs encircles the shoulder (FM 41:6).

Height: 10.4 cm, maximum diameter: 14.5 cm.

The squat-globular or biconical stirrup-jar, (FS 178, 179, 180, 181) is a typical Mycenaean pottery form, lasting from LHIIIA2 to the end of the LHIIIB period.[208] The shape is also common in Minoan pottery, with most examples dating to the LMIIIB period and a few earlier (LMIIIA2) specimens.[209]

The import of Mycenaean stirrup-jars of this shape in East Crete from the LMIIIA2 period probably led to local imitations during that and the next (LMIIIB) period, with the necessary addition of certain Minoan features. Thus, instead of the thin-thick bands that decorate the body of the imported Mycenaean stirrup-jars from Mochlos[210] and Pachyammos,[211] the Tourloti jar features the densely spaced bands of equal width that were common on Minoan stirrup-jars of this type.[212] The painter of the Tourloti jar also added the Minoan loop around the base of the neck, false spout, and handles.[213]

The shape of stirrup-jar SM 4027 closely resembles that of the LMIIIB stirrup-jars from Kritsa and Ierapetra.[214] A similar composition of hatched loops and triangles on the shoulder occurs on another contemporary stirrup-jar of the same shape and period from Stamnious Pediada, Herakleion.[215] Finally, the row of monochrome painted discs or other motifs on the shoulder is common in LH/LMIIIA2-B stirrup-jars.[216]

---

the middle LMIIIC period (Tsipopoulou and Little 2001, 86, footnote 9, 92). Thus, Tsipopoulou and Vagnetti dated the larnax with Close Style decoration from Plakalona, Tourloti, to the middle LMIIIC period (Tsipopoulou and Vagnetti 1999, 138). Furthermore, Anna Lucia D'Agata attributed the shards of the Close Octopus Style stirrup-jar from Deposit 3 at Thronos/Kefala, Amari, to the early LMIIIC period and claimed that the style appeared in Crete in this early phase (D'Agata 1999, 191, fig. 6, n. 3.20, 193-194, note 42). Macdonald dubbed 'middle LHIIIC' (= Vincent Desborough's LHIIIC1b) the period characterized by the dense octopus decoration on Rhodian stirrup-jars (Macdonald 1986, 125; Macdonald 1985, 221-224, 228). Mario Benzi agrees with Macdonald (Benzi 1992, 87). The development of the Close Style in Crete extends to the end of the LMIIIC period; see detailed discussion in Vlachopoulos 1995a, 416-433. Finally, Anna Lucia D'Agata (D'Agata 2007) disagrees with the use of the term 'middle LMIIIC' and prefers to date the contexts attributed to it to late LMIIIC, which she considers contemporary with the middle LHIIIC of mainland Greece and the Cyclades.
[208] Furumark 1941, 33, 614-615; Mountjoy 1994, 85-86, fig. 94, 113-114, fig. 130, 277.
[209] Kanta 1980, 246-248; fig. 118:2, n. HM 5372, from Episkopi, Ierapetra (LMIIIA2), fig. 20:6 and 8, n. HM 7918, from Nirou Chani (LMIIIB), fig. 20:7 and 10, n. HM 9252, from Vatheianos Kambos (LMIIIB), fig. 22:3-5, n. HM 7183, from Gournes (LMIIIB), fig. 25:3-4 and 6-7, n. HM 9887, HM 9883, from Stamnious (LMIIIB), fig. 45:1-2, 5-6, n. HM 18466, HM 18468, fig. 46:2-7, n. HM 18469, HM 18463, HM 18458, from Kalochorafitis (LMIIIB), fig. 100:5-6, 101:1-2, 5-6, from Enkomi, Cyprus (LMIIIB). Also see Bosanquet and Dawkins 1923, 102, fig. 85b, from Palaikastro (LMIIIA2); Dimopoulou and Rethemiotakis 1978, 56, 57, drawing 10, 80-82, drawing 30-31, from Metochi Kalou, Herakleion (LMIIIB); Hood, Huxley, and Sandars, 1958-1959, 242:IX 1, 249, from Ano Gypsades, Herakleion (mature LMIIIB); Tzedakis 1969, 399, fig. 7, 400 fig. 13, from Chania (LMIIIB).
[210] Banou 2005, 163 fig. 18 (LHIIIA2); Smith 2005, 193 fig. 6 (below right), 202, n. P 1073 (LHIIIB).
[211] Alexiou 1954, 403, 411, pl. H, fig. 2 (right) (LMIIIA2).
[212] Compare Kanta 1980, fig. 59:4-5, 11-12, n. HM 5370, HM 7647, from Episkopi, Ierapetra (LMIIIB); Hood, Huxley, and Sandars 1958-1959, 242, 249, n. IX.1, from Gypsades, Knossos (recent LMIIIB); Apostolakou 1998, 32-33, drawing 8, n. 12653, 44, drawing 23, n. 12674, 79-80, drawing 57, n. 12725, from Gra Lygia, Ierapetra (LMIIIB).
[213] A typical Minoan characteristic of stirrup-jars, see Kanta 1980, 248.
[214] Kanta 1980, fig. 125:8, n. 142, fig. 125:9, n. 216.
[215] Kanta 1980, fig. 25:6-7, n. HM 9883.
[216] For stirrup-jars with a similar row of dots on the shoulder, see for example Shelton 1996, 98, drawing 46, n. NAM 13992, from Prosymna (LHIIIA2); Kanta 1980, 127, fig. 115:1, n. HM 7618, from Milatos (end of

Stirrup-jar SM 4027 from Tourloti has a friable red fabric, flaky, white slip, and dull, brownish-black paint, all characteristic features of the 'Palaikstro ceramic workshop', of which numerous products have been found throughout Crete.[217] It is possible, however, that the jar comes from another local workshop with similar characteristics, active within the Mochlos-Myrsini-Tourloti triangle, as suggested by the abundance of pottery with these characteristics from these three sites.[218] Thus, the Tourloti stirrup-jar can be dated securely to the LMIIIB period and attributed to a distinctive, in its day, ceramic workshop in East Crete.

SM 4028 (ANM 4566). Globular-conical stirrup-jar (FS 175, **figs. 40-42**). Complete. Base and much of belly recomposed. Small chips on the plain, flaring rim. Occasional flaking. Fine, orange-brown fabric, same colour slip, reddish-brown paint, highly fugitive in places. Concentric circles on false spout's disc. Monochrome painted strap handles with reserved triangles on top. Painted ring on rim. Loop around base of neck and false spout. Undecorated shoulder. Three groups of thin-thick bands on body; two fine bands on lower belly.

Preserved height: 12.4 cm, maximum diameter: 10.2 cm.

The arbitrarily recomposed base was originally probably either disc- (as on stirrup-jar SM 5074) or ring-shaped. The jar's globular-conical body (FS 175) is characteristic of LH/LMIIIC stirrup-jars throughout the Aegean.[219] In East Crete, stirrup-jars of this shape have been found at Kritsa,[220] Fotoula at Praisos,[221] Tholos Tomb A at Mouliana,[222] Karfi,[223] and elsewhere. The closest parallel, however, in East Crete is a stirrup-jar from Petras, Siteia, which dates to the end of the LMIIIB or beginning of the LMIIIC period.[224] The two jars from Petras and Tourloti differ slightly in form, the first being slightly more depressed than the second. Both jars, however, have monochrome painted handles, a flat disc, and a vertical tubular neck. Also, both are decorated with similar thin-thick lines on the belly and loops around the base of the neck and false spout, according to the Helladic model.[225] Finally, both have undecorated shoulders, a rare feature in fine ceramic stirrup-jars, which occurs in the LHIIIB2 and early LHIIIC periods.[226] The Tourloti stirrup-jar probably dates to the early IIIC period and, like the Petras stirrup-jar, must come from a workshop in mainland Greece[227] or the Aegean.[228] Indeed, a group of six stirrup-jars from various sites on Skyros closely resembles the Tourloti and Petras jars. The Skyros stirrup-jars represent different variations of the globular shape, but have a fabric, slip, paint, and decoration similar

---

LMIIIB). Moreover, Kanta reports that in Crete this decorative band varies in width, and that it is characteristic in both LMIIIA and LMIIIB pottery (Kanta 1980, 251).

[217] Kanta 1980, 289; MacGillivray 1997, 198.
[218] This hypothesis, formulated by Tsipopoulou (MacGillivray 1997, 206-207), awaits confirmation after the publication of the LMIII pottery from Mochlos and the Myrsini cemetery.
[219] For the Mycenaean stirrup-jars of this shape, see Furumark 1941, 31 fig. 6, 33, 613; Mountjoy 1994, 151 (early LHIIIC), 174-176 (middle LHIIIC), 196 (late LHIIIC). For this shape in Crete, see Kanta 1980, 248.
[220] Tsipopoulou and Vagnetti 2006, 206, 210 fig. 2:a-b.
[221] Platon 1960, 304, pl. 242b (middle); Kanta 1980, 180-181, fig. 68:5.
[222] Xanthoudidis 1904, 27-28, fig. 6 (second from left); Kanta 1980, fig. 82:2, n. HM 3476.

[223] Seiradaki 1960, 16-17, fig. 11 (Type 3).
[224] Kanta 1980, 194, fig. 67:9, who dates it to the LMIIIB period.
[225] LMIII stirrup-jars usually have a complex loop around the base of the neck, false spout, and handles (Kanta 1980, 248, 250; Mountjoy 1999, 389-390, n. 70). In the LMIIIC period, several stirrup-jars, like those of the Minoan Octopus Style, lack the loop, or the loop surrounds the base of the neck and false spout only (for example Kanta 1980, fig. 116:5, n. ANM 1905, from Myrsini). In mainland Greece, the painted loop around the neck, false spout, and handles probably distinguished the 'exotic' Minoan products; added onto locally made vases, they could pass for Minoan (Paschalidis and McGeorge [forthcoming], for the 'Minoanizing Workshop' of the transitional LHIIIB2/early LMIIIC period in Western Achaea.
[226] See for example Smith 2005, 193 fig. 6 (below right), 202, n. P 1073, from Tomb 13 at Myrsini (LHIIIB); Kanta 1980, fig. 60:1-2, from Episkopi, Ierapetra (LHIIIB); Mountjoy 1999, 346, 349, n. 98, FS 167, from Pylos (early LHIIIC), 553-554, n. 257, FS 167, from the Acropolis (LHIIIB2), 683-684, n. 180, FS 174, from Thebes (early LHIIIC), 733, 734, n. 42, FS 174, from Skyros (early LHIIIC), 788, 790, n. 283, FS 175, from Phocis (late LHIIIC), 1093-1094, n. 49, FS 180, from Kos (LHIIIB).
[227] See for example Shelton 1996, 47, 339, drawing 29, n. 228; Blegen 1937, 61-62, fig. 120, n. 228, for an almost identical stirrup-jar from Tomb 20 at Prosymna (LHIIIB2).
[228] Compare the stirrup-jars from Ialysos T52/1, T71/3, T84/9 (early LHIIIC) (Benzi 1992, 342, pl. 81, 378, pl. 101, 392-393, pl. 108).

to those of stirrup-jar SM 4028 from Tourloti.[229] Thus, the attribution of the Tourloti and Petras stirrup-jars to a Skyros workshop is very tempting.[230]

The Mycenaean pottery imported in East Crete is located primarily in levels and contexts that post-date the fall of the Knossos palace, as demonstrated by the settlement and cemetery at nearby Mochlos.[231] This is often interpreted as the result of the development of local commercial and other economic relations with the Greek mainland, made possible after the collapse of Knossos's exclusive centralized control.[232] Thus, stirrup-jar SM 4028 probably ended up in a tomb at Tourloti after reaching the area as a commodity or gift during a time of free contact with Aegean markets in the postpalatial period.[233]

---

[229] Parlama 1984, 153-157, 159-160, n. 12-16, 20, pl. 66-68, 70, from Fourka, Themis, Faneromeni, and Basales, Skyros (LHIIIB2 – early LHIIIC). Also see Mountjoy 1999, 733, 734, n. 41, from Fourka, Skyros (early LHIIIC).

[230] A small Minoan stirrup-jar of the mature Octopus Style, now in the Museum of Cycladic Art (CAM 392), which allegedly comes from Skyros (Alberti and Doi 1999) sheds some more light on the island's connections with Crete in the 12th century BC. Furthermore, the vase's shape, the octopus decoration with the fringed complementary motifs on the shoulder, and the ornaments of the handles and disc cannot exclude an East Cretan origin.

[231] Smith 2005, 191, 193, fig. 6, 200-202.

[232] Smith 2005, 199. The development of contacts with mainland Greece and an intrusion of Mycenaean features in the Minoan ceramic repertoire in the Post-palatial period are noted in West Cretan sites, see for example Nezeri 2006, 12, 20.

[233] For the imported Mycenaean pottery in Crete and its significance, see Hallager 1993.

Conclusion

TOURLOTI IN THE LMIII PERIOD

Any evidence on everyday life drawn from the study of a cemetery is necessarily indirect. It is, however, a reliable source for understanding the character of a local community and of its changes through time. Because of their 'private' nature, grave gifts are often shadows of personal stories and traces of the ideologies and practices of groups and communities. Thus, the study of these three find groups from the Tourloti cemetery provides information on the site's character, history, and inhabitants during the LMIII period. This information is unfortunately patchy and can only be presented with caution.

The Tourloti cemetery is located amidst a dense network of sites, known almost exclusively from funerary finds: Lastros, Sfaka, Myrsini, and Mesa Mouliana.[234] Located near the modern road that connects the Ierapetra Isthmus with Siteia, these semi-mountainous sites belong to the territories of the homonymous modern villages. The nearby coastal settlement of Mochlos, the only site excavated thus far, is regarded, on the basis of archaeological evidence, as the portal connecting all of the above sites with the remote coastal areas of Crete, the rest of the Aegean, and Mycenaean Greece. Within this site network, Mochlos and Myrsini were probably the largest centres in the LMIIIA and LMIIIB periods. In the LMIIIC period, after the port of Mochlos was abandoned, the area's population concentrated in semi-mountainous Myrsini and Mouliana. This network of sites, each of which probably had a defined role and agricultural territory, with its internal stability and possible conflicts, was probably the major residential, commercial, and artistic centre in East Crete between Mirabello Bay and Palaikastro.[235]

Tourloti had a key place within this network of settlements. It is located between two major routes, one leading from the Mochlos port to the hinterland and the other from the LMIII town of Gournia to Palaikastro, the other major centre, on the east coast.[236] Its semi-mountainous location and ample fresh water supply ensured a self-sufficient agricultural economy for its inhabitants.[237] Moreover, the Tourloti settlement, of which no trace has been identified thus far, probably had direct commercial contacts and relations with Mycenaean Knossos towards the end of the LMIIIA1 or the beginning of the early LMIIIA2 periods. These contacts probably account for the ornate jewellery of glass, faience, and semi-precious stones, and the twelve seal stones excavated by Emmanouil Mavroeidis at Plakalona, or the small Knossian piriform jar (SM 4511) excavated by Metaxia Tsipopoulou. During the same period, the local ceramic workshops produced vases of the traditional, conservative local types, such as trefoil-spouted jug SM 4512. The presence of these two very different pottery styles within the same closed deposit at Tourloti probably reflects the different social ideologies and tendencies that coexisted east of Mycenaean Knossos during this period.

After the fall of the Knossos palace and the ensuing dissolution of its monopolies, various commodities and gifts from the rest of the Mycenaean Aegean, such as stirrup-jars SM 5073 and 5074 from North Rhodes and stirrup-jar SM 4028 possibly from Skyros, began to reach Tourloti from the beginning of the LMIIIA2 period and throughout the subsequent LMIIIB period. Exchange with the remote town of Palaikastro also continued unabated, as suggested by stirrup-jar SM 4027. Meanwhile, local ceramic workshops produced large quantities of utilitarian vessels, such as jug SM 4023, some of which, like the miniature beak-spouted jug SM 4024, were intended for funerary use.

During the early and middle LMIIIC period, Tourloti, together with Mouliana and Myrsini, probably attracted the greater part of the population that fled the coastal settlement of Mochlos. This period saw the acme of semi-mountainous

---

[234] Tsipopoulou summarized the history of the study of East Cretan LMIII sites and compiled a concise historical notice than includes all that was known up to 1995, see Tsipopoulou 1995, 177-192.

[235] As suggested by Tsipopoulou (1995, 189, 192). She also notes the possible existence of another large economic and administrative centre of the LMIIIA-B period between Petras and Achladia, Siteia, with important Mycenaean features (Tsipopoulou 2005, 309-315).

[236] One of the three Minoan roads that connected the Ierapetra Isthmus with the east coast passed through Tourloti (Pendlebury 1963, 9; Nowicki 1990, 165, pl. XXIX:a, Site 23, pl. XXX:R1, where the road from Kavousi to Siteia is marked).

[237] Nowicki 1990, 163-164.

settlements in East Crete,[238] and, although brief, it exhibits new, ambitious social structures, some of which resemble an attempt to revive the Mycenaean palatial past. From these changes came forth the new and possibly ruling class of warriors, often buried in small tholos tombs, the freestanding temple-like buildings, and the megaron-shaped structures for communal feasting, etc.[239]

The Tourloti cemetery, unlike Mouliana and Myrsini, has not produced thus far a warrior burial, a find that normally indicates the existence of a ruling class or clan. The presence, however, of the cremated remains of a young man and a (or his) child in stamnos SM 5078 suggests, at least theoretically, a will to distinguish and promote certain members of the local community through this unusual and costly burial practice, whether they were members of the settlement's ruling class or not.

This time period (early and middle LMIIIC period) is marked by the most impressive ceramic finds. The earliest of these, small figurative stirrup-jar SM 5072 with the imaginative 'magic picture' of the seabed, was manufactured by a very special artist of that region. The three Octopus Style stirrup-jars SM 5071, 4025, and 4026 are works of three different painters attached to local workshops of the Early and Close Octopus Style. These workshops distributed their products within a vast geographical area, and their painters were probably recognized and popular in the markets of that period, as discussed below. Indeed, the 'Xanthoudidis Master', to whom stirrup-jar SM 4026 from Tourloti is attributed, also painted the two famous ornate stirrup-jars from Tholos Tomb B at Mouliana, one of the earliest 'warrior burials' of the twelfth century BC in the Aegean.

Finally, the surface finds from a large, naturally fortified site at Kastri, one km southeast of the modern village of Tourloti, are also dated to the LMIIIC period. Although located too far from the Plakalona cemetery to be associated with it,[240] a major centre in this area would explain a network of surrounding cemeteries that might include the Tourloti graves. The new LMIIIC settlement at Kastri reinforces the image of the Tourloti region's temporary recovery at the end of this period and of its survival in subsequent centuries as a Doric or Eteocretan town.

---

[238] For the new, fortified sites of the LMIIIC period in the Ierapetra Isthmus and the composition of their inhabitants, see Tsipopoulou 2005, 304-306, 324.
[239] Paschalidis 2006, 222-227.
[240] Nowicki 2000, 104.

Appendix

THE TREFOIL SPOUTED JUGS 14624, 14625 AND 14626 OF THE NATIONAL ARCHAEOLOGICAL MUSEUM

NAM 14624 (BE 1970.20). Trefoil spouted jug **(figs. 43-44 left and fig. 45)**. Missing part of the spout. Small chips and white concretions in places. Almost fine, brownish-red fabric with very small white inclusions. Black paint, fugitive in places, brownish-red, fugitive slip. Narrow, cylindrical neck ending in a simple flaring rim and trefoil spout. Handle elliptical in section, attached at the rim and bottom of the shoulder. Piriform-globular body. Flat base with traces of the potter's string mark. Upper part of the vase monochrome painted, from inside the rim to the bottom of the shoulder; single drip runs the side of the belly, below the handle. Traces of the potter's wheel inside the neck and outside.

Height: 15.4 cm, maximum diameter: 12 cm, base diameter: 4.9 cm.

NAM 14625 (BE 1970.16). Trefoil spouted jug **(figs. 43-44 middle and fig. 46)**. Complete. Small chips and white concretions in places. Almost fine, brownish-red fabric with very small white inclusions. Reddish-brown paint and brownish-red slip, fugitive in places. Narrow, cylindrical neck ending in a simple flaring rim and trefoil spout. Handle elliptical in section, attached at the rim and bottom of the shoulder. Piriform-globular body. Flat base with traces of the potter's string mark. Upper part of the vase monochrome painted, from inside the rim to the bottom of the shoulder; single drip runs the side of the belly, below the handle. Traces of the potter's wheel inside the neck and outside. On the exterior, slight traces of the final surface polish. Potter's fingerprints just above the base.

Height: 14.5 cm, maximum diameter: 11.6 cm, base diameter: 5.1 cm.

NAM 14626 (BE 1970.18). Trefoil spouted jug **(figs. 43-44 right and fig. 47)**. Complete. Small chips and white concretions in places. Almost fine, pinkish-brown fabric with very small white inclusions. Fugitive reddish paint, which turns in black in places due to uneven firing. Fugitive, pinkish-brown slip. Narrow, cylindrical neck ending in a simple flaring rim and trefoil spout. Handle elliptical in section, attached at the rim and bottom of the shoulder. Piriform-globular body. Flat base with traces of the potter's string mark. Upper part of the vase monochrome painted, from inside the rim to the bottom of the shoulder; single drip runs the side of the belly below the handle. Traces of the potter's wheel inside the neck. On the exterior, slight traces of the final surface polish. Potter's fingerprints just above the base.

Height: 17.5 cm, maximum diameter: 13.1 cm, base diameter: 4.7 cm.

All three trefoil spouted jugs were confiscated by the Department of Illegal Antiquities of the Greek Police on the 31st of August 1970 and were sent to the National Archaeological Museum. They were found in Athens, in the hands of a Siteian citizen, together with a large number of other antiquities. The jugs were catalogued in the Museum's inventory volume on 11.9.1970 with the numbers: BE 1970.16, 1970.18 and 1970.20, with a note indicating that they either come from Eastern Crete or from the village of Afrati (Arkades) in Pediada, central Crete.

The NAM 14624, 14625 and 14626 jugs share a number of common elements with each other, such as fabric, shape, decoration (upper part monochrome painted, same drip of paint below handle), and technique (same traces of potter's wheel and string marks, potter's finger-prints similarly applied around the base), that should be regarded as the products of the same workshop, if not of the same person. By contrast, the Tourloti trefoil spouted jug (SM 4512) has a rather circular handle section and also differs in the position of the drip of paint, which is not below the handle, but rather on the side of the vase. Still, the rest of the jug's main features are so significantly similar, that it should be accepted as another product of the above mentioned workshop. As already discussed in Chapter I, this potter's workshop should have been active within the Tourloti-Mochlos-Myrsini area.

All four jugs bear finger-prints similarly applied around the base, as already mentioned. These can be explained as the traces of the potter's hands holding the vases upside down in order to dip them in paint. The vases were then lifted upright and slightly inclined, so that a sole drip ran from the handle - or the shoulder - to the belly.

Chapter II

STIRRUP-JAR SM 4026, THE 'XANTHOUDIDIS MASTER', AND THE OCTOPUS STYLE IN EAST CRETE

SM 4026 (ANM 4564). Globular stirrup-jar (FS 176, **pls. 4a, 4b and figs. 48-53**). Complete, except for the base, which was probably ring-shaped. Surface chipped and flaked in places. Pinkish-red fabric with many small inclusions. Orange-brown slip, reddish-brown paint, highly fugitive in places. Left-spinning spiral on the slightly concave disc. Strap handles monochrome painted on the sides. Painted ring on the flaring rim; three painted stripes on the cylindrical neck. Wide rings around the base of the neck, false spout, and handles. Wide and narrow bands decorate the lower body. An ornate, stylized octopus (FM 21) occupies the upper body and shoulder. Four tentacles grow out of the head, which is located below the neck, spiral over the entire surface, and meet on the backside. Monochrome painted discs framed by concentric circles denote the eyes. Monochrome painted 'egg' on the forehead. The fringed upper tentacles and the lower two pairs of tentacles end in multiple spiralling stems (FM 19). The fourth and largest pair of tentacles spreads symmetrically along the decorative panel and ends in two large spirals on the back. Between these two spirals is a peculiar eye-like ornament, formed by consecutive fringed and linear arches framing a leaf-shaped motif. Short lines and groups of arches with pendant U-shaped motifs (FM 45) fill the spaces between the tentacles. Rows of U-shaped motifs also decorate the panel's base. Finally, two four-petaled flowers, or 'sea anemones', decorate the shoulder on either side of the neck (FM 27:47).

Preserved height: 16.2 cm, maximum diameter: 16.3 cm

Like stirrup jar SM 4025, SM 4026 from Tourloti is a typical example of the globular stirrup-jars of the Minoan Close Octopus Style and dates to the middle LMIIIC period. Despite its generally poor state of preservation, SM 4026 preserves enough morphological and decorative features that allow it to contribute significantly to the discussion on the workshops of Octopus Style vases and larnakes in East Crete.

The closest parallel for SM 4026 is provided by the two Close Octopus Style stirrup-jars from Tholos Tomb B at Sellades, Mesa Mouliana, a few kilometres east of Tourloti (**figs. 54-57 and 58-61**).[241] Undisturbed until its investigation by Stefanos Xanthoudidis in February 1903,[242] this small tomb with square ground plan and vaulted roof contained the burials of two warriors of the LMIIIC period.[243] One of the deceased had been placed inside a tub larnax, while the other lay on the floor. Next to the latter's head were the two stirrup-jars mentioned above.

The two stirrup-jars from Tholos Tomb B at Mouliana share the same globular shape (FS 176), ring base, short strap handles, slightly concave disc, short, narrow, cylindrical neck, and funnel-shaped rim. Xanthoudidis reports that one was taller than the other by a few centimetres, that both jars had the same "fine, red fabric" and "red and brown" paint. Their decoration is also very similar: wide and narrow bands are arranged in a similar manner on the lower body, similar horizontal brushstrokes decorate the necks, and similar fine, well executed spirals fill the discs.

The main decorative panel on both jars depicts an octopus, arranged in a similar manner and with the same aesthetic approach. Broad, wavy bands framed by thin lines denote the tentacles, which sprawl and curl in the same flowing manner and are interconnected by the same complementary ornaments. However, whereas the octopus head and body dominate the front of one stirrup-jar (HM 3480, **figs. 54, 57**), they are omitted entirely from the other (HM 3481, **fig. 61**) and replaced by the tentacles' spiralling tips, as on the back. Moreover, the composition of the latter stirrup-jar is slightly denser than that of the former.

The same remarks can be made of the shape, fabric, paint, and decoration on the lower body, handles, disc, and neck of stirrup-jar SM 4026 from Tourloti, which is a few centimetres shorter than

---

[241] Kanta 1980, 175, 255, fig. 82: 5-6 (n. HM 3480), 82: 8-9 (n. HM 3481); Xanthoudidis 1904, 42-43, where stirrup-jars n. 1-2 are listed, 43-44, fig. 10 (right and middle), for a photograph of the jars, and pl. 1, for layouts of the octopus compositions (jar n. 1 above and n. 2 below). Stirrup-jar HM 3480 from Mouliana is frequently cited as a typical example of the Close Octopus Style in Minoan pottery, see for example Desborough 1964, pl. 6a; Popham 1967, 347, 349, pl. 89d; Betancourt 1985, 184 fig. 131; Popham 1994, 101; pl. 12g.

[242] Xanthoudidis 1904, 38-50.

[243] For the expression 'warrior tombs' in the LH/LMIIIC period, see Paschalidis and McGeorge (forthcoming).

the Mouliana jars. Despite its poorly preserved surface, it was possible to reconstruct the octopus composition and to compare it with that of the Mouliana jars. The great similarity in the organisation of the composition and in the aesthetic conception of the main decorative panels on all three jars is obvious.

Stirrup-jar SM 4026 from Tourloti depicts an octopus similar to the one on the first Mouliana jar (HM 3480). The painter rendered the animal's head and body in a similar manner, but included all eight tentacles (instead of six as on the Mouliana jar) and filled the space on either side of the neck with two four-petaled flowers, or 'sea anemones' (FM 27:47), instead of the fringed seashells (FM 25) of jar HM 3480. These four-petaled flowers were also used on the second Mouliana jar (HM 3481). Moreover, the complementary motifs of the Tourloti jar also appear on the Mouliana jars, squeezed in between the tentacles in a similar manner. Finally, the close similarity between the enigmatic eye-like ornaments on the backside of the Tourloti stirrup-jar (**figs. 51, 53**) and jar HM 3480 from Mouliana (**fig. 57**) is impressive. Framed by fringes and pendant U-shaped motifs, these ornaments do not occur in any other octopus composition of the twelfth century BC in the Aegean.

A fourth Close Octopus Style stirrup-jar, now in the Museum of Cycladic Art (N. P. Goulandris Foundation, CAM 484), is very similar to the above three and allegedly comes from Siteia (**pls. 3a, 3b and figs. 62, 63**).[244] The Goulandris stirrup-jar is slightly larger than the Tourloti jar (SM 4026) and slightly smaller than the Mouliana jars (HM 3480 and 3481). It features the same globular body (FS 176), ring base, short strap handles, flat disc, short, narrow, cylindrical neck, and funnel-shaped rim. The wide and narrow bands covering its lower body are identical to those of the Tourloti and Mouliana jars. The sides of the handles are monochrome painted as on the Tourloti jar, but lack the transversal lines of the Mouliana jars. Finally, the pinkish-red fabric and reddish-brown paint are the same as on the Tourloti and, possibly, the Mouliana jars.

The painted decoration on the Goulandris stirrup-jar (CAM 484) is most interesting. Instead of an octopus, the main decorative panel on the shoulder depicts a single tentacle winding its way across the surface to form four full, symmetrical waves. Two thin lines underline the tentacle, and U-shaped motifs along its upper edge recall the octopus' suckers. 'Sea anemones' (FM 26:47) and consecutive arches crowned by U-shaped motifs fill the space below the tentacle.

All of the above decorative features appear in a similar manner on stirrup-jars SM 4026 from Tourloti and HM 3480 from Mouliana. However, the Goulandris stirrup-jar's likeness to jar HM 3481 from Mouliana is even more striking, and Colin Macdonald considers these two jars virtual twins.[245] Certain differences, however, are worth pointing out. The complementary ornaments in the spaces above the tentacles do not occur on either of the Mouliana or the Tourloti jars. Of these ornaments, the two eight-petaled rosettes and the single four-petaled rosette are common in this period's repertoire.[246] The main complementary motif, however, below the neck, is unique. It represents a pendant ivy leaf (FM 12) with diminishing parallel strokes framing the stem, all of which recalls the papyrus-like flowers of LMIIIA and LMIIIB vase painting.[247] This peculiar motif resembles to some extent the two rather simpler, more stylized 'flowers', painted on earlier vases from Gra Lygia in Ierapetra and Knossos.[248]

The Goulandris stirrup-jar also differs from the Mouliana and Tourloti jars in other respects. It lacks the horizontal lines that decorate the neck of

---

[244] Doumas and Marangou 1978, 164; Marangou 1996, 39 n. 19, fig. 18.

[245] Macdonald was the first to note the close similarity between stirrup-jars CAM 484 and HM 3481, without further discussion (Macdonald 1985, 228). Vlachopoulos (1995, 425-426) discussed this similarity too and attributed the Mouliana vases HM 3480, HM 3481 and the Goulandris stirrup-jar to the same artist.
[246] See for example the stirrup-jar from Kritsa (Kanta 1980, fig. 136:1).
[247] Apostolakou 1998, 82, drawing 60, on a larnax from Gra Lygia, Ierapetra (LMIIIA2); Kanta 1980, fig. 75:2, on a small piriform jar from Sklavoi, Siteia (LMIIIB), fig. 119:1, on a stirrup-jar from Kalochorafitis Mesara (LMIIIA2 or early LMIIIB), fig. 140:1, on a piriform jar from Episkopi, Ierapetra (LMIIIA2 or early LMIIIB); Warren 1997, 180, fig. 36 (third row, on the right), on a cup from the excavation behind the Stratigraphical Museum at Knossos (LMIIIB); Alexiou 1967, pl. 6, on the famous beak-spouted jug from Katsambas, Herakleion, where the papyrus flower is pendant as on the Goulandris jar (LMIIIA1).
[248] Apostolakou 1998, 59, drawing 40, n. 12695, note 174, from Gra Lygia, Ierapetra (LMIIIA2); Popham 1967, 348, fig. 6:2, from Knossos (LMIIIB).

the other three jars, and features a painted 'hourglass' with multiple outlines instead of the usual spiral on the disc. Whether painted or in reserve on a monochrome painted ground, the 'hourglass' is characteristic of Cretan stirrup-jars and occurs on the disc of several examples of the LMIIIB and LMIIIC periods.[249] This motif appears on another small stirrup-jar of the mature Octopus Style, now also in the Museum of Cycladic Art (CAM 392) and possibly from East Crete.[250]

Finally, although the Goulandris stirrup-jar's fabric and paint resemble those of the Mouliana and Tourloti jars, its slip is yellowish and glossy, an unusual feature for East Cretan pottery, though common in the Pediada and West Crete. Yellowish and quite glossy, however, is the slip on the fragmented Octopus Close Style stirrup-jar SM 4025 from the Fygetakis submission, a vase which has already been attributed to an East Cretan workshop.

On the basis of the macroscopic and aesthetic observations cited above,[251] stirrup-jars SM 4026 from Tourloti and HM 3480 and HM 3481 from Mouliana can be attributed with some certainty to the same workshop and indeed to the same painter, whom we have conventionally dubbed the 'Xanthoudidis Master'. Because of its poignant morphological and stylistic similarities, stirrup-jar CAM 484 can be added to this group of vases with some reservation.

Although the accuracy and usefulness of distinguishing workshops and painters in Mycenaean and Minoan pottery have been questioned,[252] this study upholds the obvious value of recognizing individual elements in antiquity, particularly when these can be viewed against the general anonymity of the mundane arts at the borders of the prehistoric Aegean at the end of the Bronze Age.

Stefanos Xanthoudidis, who excavated the Mouliana tholos tombs, did much more than simply provide a detailed publication of the excavation process and its finds. Even though the archaeology of prehistoric Crete was still nascent and the various chapters of the knowledge that is now taken for granted were not even hypothetically formulated when he wrote his report in 1903, Xanthoudidis considered the origins, use, and significance of the clay larnakes from the Cretan tombs[253] and even the significance and development of the octopus motif on Cretan stirrup-jars.[254] He displayed the same care and interest when dealing with the architecture of the tombs, the location of the deceased and their grave gifts, etc. Despite certain erroneous conclusions, such as the attribution of the two Mouliana stirrup-jars (HM 3480 and 3481) to two different stages of development of the octopus motif, his interest in the representation of the octopus on 'ceramic monuments' makes him a pioneer in the history of the study of this motif.[255]

---

[249] Popham 1965, 319, fig. 1, 320, pl. 82d, n. K44, N46; Andreadaki-Vlazaki and Papadopoulou 2005, 386, fig. 50, from Chamalevri, Rethymno (LMIIIC); Kanta 1980, fig. 120:1 and 3, from Kritsa (LMIIIB); Apostolakou 1998, 46-48, drawing 28, 51-52, drawing 32, from Gra Lygia, Ierapetra, but manufactured in Kydonia (LMIIIB); Hallager 2003, 149, pl. 57, n. 70-P0745, from Kastelli, Chania (LMIIIB2); Tzedakis 1969, 413, fig. 33, from Chania (LMIIIB); Mountjoy 1999, pl. 8:f, from Ialysos, but manufactured in Crete (LMIIIC).

[250] Alberti and Doi 1999. According to the Museum of Cycladic Art archives, the vase came from Skyros. Its shape, however, the octopus with the fringed complementary motifs on the shoulder, and the decoration of the handles and disc suggest a Cretan origin and a date in the period of the mature Close Octopus Style.

[251] No petrographic or chemical analysis of the fabric was carried out. Information on the Mouliana stirrup-jars was based on published photographs and descriptions by the excavator and later scholars. It was not possible to examine and re-photograph the jars, because of the ongoing renovation of the Herakleion Archaeological Museum, during which the storerooms are closed.

[252] For the history of the identification of painters and workshops in the prehistoric Aegean and the uncertainty of its accuracy and usefulness, see for example Thomas 1997, 377-378, 381-382; Vlachopoulos 2006, 159-163; Paschalidis 2001, 103-104. Spyridon Iakovidis, Joost Crowel, Colin Macdonald, Emily Vermeule, Vassos Karageorghis, and others have distinguished painters of stirrup-jars in the past (Vlachopoulos 1995, 255, note 57 and Vlachopoulos 1995a, 424-427). In recent years, Vlachopoulos distinguished a number of painters of the Close Octopus Style, who were active in Naxos (Vlachopoulos 2006, 163-187) and Tiryns (Vlachopoulos, 2006a). Finally, Tsipopoulou and Vagnetti presented, among others, the painter of four larnakes and one stirrup-jar of the Octopus Style in East Crete (Tsipopoulou and Vagnetti 1997). For identification of larnax painters and workshops of the LMIII period and the distribution of their products, see Merousis 2000, 408-411.

[253] Xanthoudidis 1904, 10-17.
[254] Xanthoudidis 1904, 43-47.
[255] Xanthoudidis 1904, 45-46. Angelo Mosso's slightly later treatment of the subject is also interesting (Mosso 1907, 210).

With his monograph *Cretan Civilization*, the first systematic handbook on Minoan civilization since the foundation of the Cretan State, Xanthoudidis contributed significantly to the promotion of the newly established archaeology of Crete.[256] The book included a lengthy chapter on the art of ceramics and its known styles, including the octopus motif.[257] The identification of stirrup-jars SM 4026 from Tourloti, HM 3480 and HM 3481 from Mouliana, and CAM 484 of the Goulandris Collection as works of the same painter would not be easy today had not Xanthoudidis approached the finds from his excavation with such care and close documentation and showed a genuine interest in compiling the knowledge of the new science of archaeology.[258]

The activity of the 'Xanthoudidis Master' belongs to the rich production of the East Cretan ceramic workshops of the Close Octopus Style. Despite the technical and stylistic similarities, as noted in the pottery catalogue above, between the Fygetakis stirrup-jar SM 4025 and those attributed to the 'Xanthoudidis Master' (globular body [FS 176], combined thin-thick bands, steadiness in the use of the fine paintbrush, precise rendering of the main decorative motif [octopus]), the former jar's poor state of preservation does not allow further stylistic connections with the Master's work. The jar (SM 4025) can, however, be attributed with certainty to an East Cretan workshop.

The four stirrup-jars of the 'Xanthoudidis Master' are comparable with three other Close Octopus Style jars of East Cretan manufacture found outside Crete: the Minoan stirrup-jar from Aplomata in Naxos and the two stirrup-jars from Ialysos in Rhodes.

Stirrup-jar NM 914 from Aplomata (**figs. 64-66**), which Chrysoula Kardara attributed to a Cretan workshop and compared with stirrup-jar HM 3480 from Mouliana, has a similar shape (FS 176), but different fabric and paint.[259] The arrangement of the decoration is similar to that of the 'Xanthoudidis Master' jars, with thin-thick bands decorating the jar's lower half, from the base until a little above the maximum diameter, and an octopus with complementary motifs occupying the shoulder. Moreover, the 'sea anemones' (FM 27:47) on either side of the Aplomata jar occur on three of the four 'Xanthoudidis Master' jars. The addition, however, of a bird on the backside of the Aplomata specimen, an unusual motif for Minoan octopus vases,[260] and, more particularly, the composition's overall style suggest a different artist of the mid-LMIIIC period, who maintained certain stylistic affinities with the 'Xanthoudidis Master' and therefore may have also worked in East Crete.

The Octopus Style stirrup-jars T 87/3 and T15/2 from Ialysos were promptly identified as Cretan products and repeatedly compared with the Mouliana jar (HM 3480). The analytical examination of their fabric further supported the hypothesis of a Minoan, possibly East Cretan origin.[261] Stirrup-jar T87/3's (**pl. 4d left**) slightly depressed globular shape (FS 176) and painted composition of octopus and complementary motifs[262] recall those of the 'Xanthoudidis Master' group. The Ialysos jar, however, features a vertical row of hatched lozenges on the backside, instead of the characteristic eye-shaped ornament. Moreover, the overall composition suggests an earlier that the 'Xanthoudidis Master' stage of the Close Octopus Style, in the early LMIIIC period.[263]

---

[256] Xanthoudidis 1904a. Stefanos Xanthoudidis used the expression 'Cretan' to designate finds from pre-Hellenic Crete, thus reacting to the term 'Mycenaean', which was more widely accepted in his day (Xanthoudidis 1904a, 3-4). Arthur Evans eventually replaced the term 'Mycenaean' with the term 'Minoan' a few years later, see Seager 1912, 3; Zois 1996, 257-280.

[257] Xanthoudidis 1904a, 76-83.

[258] For Xanthoudidis's life and work, see Oikonomos 1928, 7-9; Oikonomos 1928a, 628-634; Georgiadis 1940; Detorakis 1990; Kopaka 2002.

[259] Kardara 1977, 18-19, drawing 8, pl. 20, 21a. Vlachopoulos also considers it Cretan and related it to Octopus Style examples of the middle LMIIIC from Central and East Crete, see Vlachopoulos 2006, 337, 338: fig. 93, pl. 106, colour pl. 7 (below) and Vlachopoulos 1995a, 426.

[260] Macdonald 1986, 136.

[261] Kanta 1980, 305, fig. 100:1-2; Macdonald 1985, 214; Macdonald 1986, 136; Benzi 1992, 6, 10, 87-88, pl. 15c, 110b-c.

[262] Benzi 1992, 76, 396.

[263] Kanta recognized early LMIIIC features on both stirrup-jars from Ialysos (Kanta 1980, 305). By contrast, Macdonald dates them to the middle LMIIIC period (Macdonald 1985, 222). Mountjoy included them in the Minoan stirrup-jars from Ialysos and dates them to the early LHIIIC – middle (developed) LHIIIC period (Mountjoy 1999, 1046, 1051, pl. 6e-f, 8a-b). Vlachopoulos also dates them to the early LHIIIC period (Vlachopoulos 2006a, 189).

Stirrup-jar T15/2 from Ialysos (**pl. 4d right**) has the same globular shape (FS 176).[264] The octopus' shape resembles greatly those on stirrup-jars HM 3480 from Mouliana and SM 4026 from Tourloti, despite the differences in the complementary motifs, particularly on the back. The arrangement of the bands on the lower body,[265] however, and the somewhat loose composition of the main decorative panel suggest an early LMIIIC date for this jar also. Metaxia Tsipopoulou and Lucia Vagnetti recently attributed stirrup-jar T15/2 from Ialysos to the 'Petras-Piskokefalo Group Master', who specialized primarily in the manufacture and decoration of larnakes and who was active in East Crete, between Siteia and Kritsa, in the early LMIIIC period.[266]

Siteia, Tourloti, and Mesa Mouliana, where the 'Xanthoudidis Master' was active, were all within the range of the 'Petras-Piskokefalo Group Master'. According to current data, the former potter specialized in stirrup-jars only, whereas the latter manufactured both larnakes and stirrup-jars. The two potters' octopus designs are very similar, as demonstrated by the comparison of larnax 23436 now in the Museum of Art and History in Geneva (**fig. 67**) and stirrup-jar T15/2 from Ialysos (**pl. 4d right**) with stirrup-jars SM 4026 from Tourloti (**pls. 4a, 4b and figs. 48-53**) and HM 3480 from Mouliana (**figs. 54-57**). Their compositions show the same clarity and steadiness of the lines, the same symmetry in the development of the decorative subject, and the same preference for spiralling tips for the tentacles and other lines. The bodies of all of the octopuses develop with the same consistency along the vertical axis. The large monochrome painted eyes, central 'egg', and fringed crown are common in all works. The main dividing line between the works of these two potters is ultimately their period of activity, the 'Petras-Piskokefalo Group Master' having been active in the early LMIIIC period and the 'Xanthoudidis Master' in the middle LMIIIC period. But how reliable are these chronological 'silhouettes'?

The 'Xanthoudidis Master' vases are dated on the basis of style (Close Octopus Style) and the study of finds from the same contexts. The latter can only take into account the two stirrup-jars from Tholos Tomb B at Mouliana (HM 3480 and 3481), since both SM 4026 from Tourloti and CAM 484 of the Goulandris collection have no context, the former being a submission and the latter a purchase from the antiquities' market. Thus, a brief re-examination of the context of two of the 'Xanthoudidis Master' vases is required.

Mouliana's Tholos Tomb B contained two burials, one in a tub larnax and another on the floor. The two stirrup-jars HM 3480 and HM 3481 were placed next to the head of the body that lay on the floor.[267] The deceased had a type Naue II A2 (according to Imma Kilian-Dirlmeier's classification)[268] sword on his left side and wore a peculiar 'mask' made of a rectangular gold sheet. The excavator mentions two more stirrup-jars, the location of which 'between this body and the larnax' and 'at the bottom end of the larnax' makes their association with the deceased on the floor doubtful.[269] The two copper alloy spearheads found outside the larnax probably belong to the deceased on the floor.[270] Of the grave gifts that can be securely associated with this burial, the gold 'mask' is unique,[271] the two Close Octopus Style stirrup-jars are dated to the middle LMIIIC period on stylistic grounds, one of the two spearheads with Central European characteristics is dated to the LHIIIB2 period,[272] and the type Naue II A2 sword

---

[264] Mauri 1923-1924, 172 fig. 99 (below right), pl. II (n. 3155); Benzi 1992, 76, 251, pl. 15c.
[265] Compare with octopus stirrup-jar SM 5071 from the Papadakis excavation.
[266] Kanta was the first to identify and date the activity of the painter of the larnakes from Tourtouloi, Piskokefalo, and Petras (Kanta 1980, 292, fig. 65:3-4, 66:1-2, 73:9-10). Tsipopoulou and Vagnetti added to the group the larnax of the Musée d'Art et d'Histoire in Geneva inv.n. 23436 and stirrup-jar T15/2 from Ialysos (Tsipopoulou and Vagnetti 1997, 474 ff). For the relation between larnax painters and vase painters, and for octopuses and their symbolism on Minoan larnakes, see Merousis 2000, 257-267, 406.

[267] Xanthoudidis 1904, 39-44.
[268] Kilian-Dirlmeier 1993, 95, pl. 34, n. 230.
[269] Only one of these two stirrup-jars is pictured in the excavation report and not very clearly (Xanthoudidis 1904, 43-44, fig. 10 left).
[270] These spearheads probably belonged to the deceased on the floor, since the other deceased's rich weaponry was found with him inside the larnax. Unfortunately, the excavator does not report the location of the spearheads in relation to the floor burial (Xanthoudidis 1904, 45-46, fig. 11, 48).
[271] For the Mouliana 'mask' and the gold plaques covering the face of the deceased in the prehistoric Aegean, see Vlachopoulos 2006, 280 ff.
[272] Höckmann, 1980, 69, fig. 15, 67-76, for Type K and its third variant, in which Höckmann classifies the spearhead with 'Central European' features from Tomb

is dated on typological grounds to the LHIIIB2/early LHIIIC period.[273] Thus, the second warrior of Tholos Tomb B at Mouliana was probably buried in the early LMIIIC period or, at the latest, in the beginning of the middle LMIIIC period, provided of course that the sword and spearhead were acquired by him and were not heirlooms transmitted from generation to generation.

The Close Octopus Style stirrup-jars from Tholos Tomb B and the overall activity of the 'Xanthoudidis Master' can therefore be dated accordingly between the early and middle LMIIIC periods.[274] The common iconographic and stylistic language of the 'Petras-Piskokefalo Group' and 'Xanthoudidis' masters and the close proximity of when they were active, demonstrated by the above examination, might even suggest that they both worked in the same workshop, roughly one generation apart.

If this is indeed the case, we are dealing with a long-lived East Cretan 'workshop'[275] that produced larnakes and stirrup-jars with octopuses – that is, ornate objects intended for funerary use[276] – sent to markets from Kritsa to Petras and from Piskokefalo to Ialysos in Rhodes.[277] In fact, the vases of the 'Xanthoudidis Master' were chosen to accompany one of the earliest Aegean 'warrior burials' of the twelfth century BC.[278] The painter of the Fygetakis stirrup-jar (SM 4025, **figs. 34-36**) might also be associated with this 'workshop'. It is also tempting to include as products of the same 'workshop' the two ornate stirrup-jars of the mature Close Octopus and Fringed Style of the middle LMIIIC period from Room 4 in Building B at Kavousi-Vronda,[279] of which the obvious similarities in specific morphological and stylistic features suggest a 'local school' rather than mere coincidence (**fig. 68**).[280]

B at Mouliana, and 150, n. K27. Jan Bouzek also sees close similarities between the two Mouliana spearheads and European types (Bouzek 1985, 137, 138, 141).

[273] Two of the other three swords of early Type Naue II Group A found in the Aegean and Cyprus (Langada in Kos and Enkomi) are securely dated to the end of the LHIIIB and early LHIIIC periods (Kilian-Dirlmeier 1993, 100, notes 17, 18). The Myrsini tomb and the context in which the third sword was found are still unpublished (Kilian-Dirlmeier 1993, 95 n. 227); the sword's exact date is thus unknown. Two more swords of the so-called 'early' Type Naue II Group A, which date, however, to the late LHIIIC period, were recently found at Voudeni and Spaliarelika-Lousika (Jung, Moschos, and Mehofer [forthcoming]).

[274] D'Agata (D'Agata 2007, 9, 113, fig. 13) erroneously identified the stirrup-jar from Tomb B (HM 3480) with the stirrup-jar from Tholos Tomb A at Mouliana (HM 3476), mistaking the photograph published by Xanthoudidis (Xanthoudidis 1904, 27-28, fig. 6). Thus, she dated the 'Master's' vase incorrectly to the late, instead of the middle, LMIIIC period, on the basis of other finds from Tomb A. Xanthoudidis's precise description, however, of the finds from both graves and the photographs published by Kanta leave no doubt as to which vase belongs to which tomb (Xanthoudidis 1904, 26-28, 32-36 [Tomb A], 42-47 [Tomb B]; Kanta 1980, fig. 82:2-3, 5-6). Thus, stirrup-jar HM 3480 was found inside Tomb B, associated with the early/middle LMIIIC burial on the floor, whereas stirrup-jar HM 3476 was found inside Tomb A, on the left as one enters, together with other objects of the middle and late LMIIIC period (three Close Style stirrup-jars, Type F and Type Naue II C3 swords, bow fibulae, and fragments of copper-alloy vessels).

[275] Here the term 'worshop' designated the pottery production of a region and its common decorative features, rather than a specific manufacturing center. For the term 'workshop' in the Mycenaean Aegean, see Vlachopoulos 2006, 159, and Merousis 2000, 410.

[276] According to Vlachopoulos, the small number of richly decorated Octopus Style stirrup-jars compared to the total of twelfth-century BC Naxian pottery confirms the hypothesis that these vases were prestige objects, intended to be used as grave gifts rather than in daily life (Vlachopoulos 2006, 151, note 9; Vlachopoulos 1995, 255).

[277] According to Macdonald, LMIIIC Crete exported liquid goods to Rhodes packaged in stirrup-jars or Octopus Style stirrup-jars, sold *per se* for their artistic qualities and funerary use (Macdonald 1986, 149). Xanthoudidis, however, notes the "Mouliana wine", famous to this day in East Crete (Xanthoudidis 1904, 22).

[278] For the term 'warrior tombs' in the LHIIIC period and the importance of Type Naue II swords in their development, see Paschalidis and McGeorge (forthcoming). For the LMIII Cretan 'warrior tombs', see Driessen and Macdonald 1984; Kanta 2003; Tsipopoulou 2005, 327-329, with a commentary on Tombs A and B at Mouliana.

[279] Preston Day 1997, 395-398, fig. 4:1-3; D'Agata 2007, 93, 107, fig. 4, for the stirrup-jars with octopuses from Building B, Room 4, at Kavousi-Vronda, which belong to the settlement's Phase I (early - middle LMIIIC period), contemporary with Phase II on the Kastro at Kavousi (personal communication with Dr Preston Day).

[280] The East Cretan potters's marked preference for the 'heavy', globular body with short handles, neck, and false spout (FS 176) contrasts with that of the Attic and Naxian workshops for globular-biconical shapes (FS 175). This group of East Cretan vases also shows a similar distribution of the field (bands on the lower half, a pictorial composition on the upper half) and other

Finally, three more Close Style stirrup-jars from Kritsa **(fig. 69)**,[281] Vasiliki in Ierapetra **(fig. 70)**,[282] and Thronos/Kefala in Amari **(fig. 71)**[283] might be attributed to a single East Cretan 'master', active in the early LMIIIC period and who maintained some relation to the 'workshop' of the 'Xanthoudidis' and Petras-Piskokefalo Group' masters.[284]

In any case, East Crete was probably the most active production centre of high quality painted pottery on the entire island in the twelfth century BC.[285] Its Octopus Style stirrup-jars and larnakes were widely distributed in Central and West Crete, the Dodecanese, and the Cyclades.[286] This impressive distribution underlines their high quality and suggests that they were recognized as products with 'label of origin'. The 'Xanthoudidis Master', whose characteristic style was his work's 'trademark', was a dynamic figure in the ceramic art of his time.

---

morphological and stylistic similarities, such as the strap handles, vertical neck, base, U-shaped outlines of the circles and spirals, etc, which suggest a 'school' of Octopus/Fringed Style stirrup-jars active in the middle LMIIIC period.

[281] Kanta 1980, 255, fig. 136:1, n. HM 180.
[282] Kanta 1980, 255; Popham 1967, pl. 89ff.
[283] D'Agata 1999, 191, fig. 6:3.20, 193-194. D'Agata dated the stirrup-jar shards from Thronos/Kefala to early LMIIIC on the basis of the closed context from the excavation's Votive Pit 3. The group's two stirrup-jars from Kritsa and Vasiliki can be dated to the same period.
[284] The similarities concern the vases' globular shape (FS 176) and certain morphological features in the octopus design, which occur primarily in the 'Xanthoudidis Master' and which can be the object of a separate discussion.
[285] For East Crete's pioneering role in the creation and development of the Close and Fringed Styles, see Popham 1994, 101.
[286] For the wide distribution of the larnakai produced in East Cretan workshop, see Merousis 2000, 408-410, with bibliography.

Chapter III

THE CREMATION BURIAL FROM PLAKALONA, TOURLOTI

P.J.P. McGeorge

Introductory Remarks

The vase on display in the Siteia Museum (**fig. 72**) was excavated twenty-five years ago in a Late Minoan III rock-cut tomb at Plakalona Tourloti by N. Papadakis, who reported it briefly in the 1984 *Arch Delt*. It contains a cremation burial that curiously was not mentioned in the report.

Cremation burial is unusual at this period, though not unknown. In the cemetery at Tourloti, it is so far unique. The origin of the rite of cremation at this date is a subject of debate. Cremation became common practice later, in the Geometric period, replacing the earlier rite of inhumation burial usual in the Bronze Age, and it probably reflects the beginning of a change in people's religious beliefs, of which the Tourloti burial is an early example, paralleled by a scatter of contemporary instances of cremations known at other sites on Crete.

General Observations

The vase, which is of a coarse fabric, its surface flaked and severely weathered, is preserved to about half its original height and probably contains only a portion of its original contents, which turned out to be a double cremation. The bones from it weighed 495 gm, approximately one third of the expected weight of the remains of an adult cremated in a modern furnace, which reduces a skeleton to dust. Ancient cremation techniques would not have been so efficient consequently one might expect a greater volume of bone, but this is not the case at Tourloti. Some remains could have been lost due to post-depositional circumstances, in this case the partial collapse of the tomb, but it could be that people were either not too meticulous or not particularly enthusiastic about collecting bones from the pyre.

The bones in the Tourloti cremation were considerably warped and extensively fissured, but large diagnostic fragments survived. However, these did not include very much of the leg bones, although one would have expected the denser parts of the femurs such as the ball joints to have survived the pyre. The bones are mainly white coloured, but in a few places there are areas of grey and black, specifically noted on the back of the skull and the back of the scapula and some wrist bones. These less well burnt areas suggest that the body, as one would expect, was probably laid out supine on the pyre. These grey black pieces also suggest that the temperature of the pyre did not exceed 900 degrees centigrade. There are some patches of a brown substance adhering to the surface of the humerus.

The relatively large size of the bone fragments suggests that the remains were not pounded, although we cannot exclude the possibility that bone dust could have been lost during the cleaning of the vase, before the cremation was replaced in it and put on display.

Included amongst the human bones from the remains of the pyre, probably accidentally, was a small fragment of a sheep/goat premolar, perhaps part of a funerary feast.

Skeletal Parts Present

Adult

This is an adult male of 25 years. While the supra orbital margins do not appear particularly male, the nuchal crest development of the occipital enables a positive determination of male sex. The surviving fragments of the humeri also do not appear particularly male, but as there is no duplication of adult anatomical parts it is concluded that a single adult individual is buried here.

Cranium:
1] Right frontal with sharp orbital margin (**fig. 73**)
2] Right zygomatic with lateral margin of the right orbit (**fig. 73**)
3] An occipital fragment with prominent *protuberantia occpitalis interna* and marked nuchal crest development, for the attachments of muscles to support the weight of a large, diagnostically male skull. The lambdoid sutures were not fused on either surface (**fig. 74**).
4] Basi-occipital synchondrosis which is fused indicating an adult of 20-25 +years (**fig.75**)
5] Both pars petrosa (**fig. 75**).
6] Sphenoid (**fig. 75**)
7] Right temporal bone with condylar notch (**fig. 76**)
8] Right sphenoid fragment - the temporal-sphenoid sutures were not fused.

Mandible & Teeth:
9] Right mandible condyle **(fig. 76)**
10] Left ascending ramus with left coronoid and condyle **(fig. 76)**

Tooth roots **(fig. 77)**:
11] Upper I 2s
12] Upper left M2 & M3
13] Lower incisors
14] Lower left canine
15] Double rooted pre-molar
16] Several molar roots

Post Cranial Remains:
17] Right clavicle shaft fragment **(fig. 78)**
18] Left clavicle shaft fragment **(fig. 79)**
19] Left scapula with glenoid & spine **(fig. 80)**
20] R humerus, biepicondylar breadth=50mm+ **(fig. 81)**
21] L humerus head diameter=42 mm, shaft **(figs. 81-82)**
22] Left radius distal articulation, width=26 mm **(fig. 83)**
23] Left radius proximal articulation width=27.1 mm **(fig. 83)**
24] Proximal right radius **(fig. 83)**
25] Distal right radius **(fig. 83)**
26] Carpals: scaphoid W=23.9mm; capitate w= 21.2mm; lunate ht=14.5mm trapezium ht=21.2mm, w=15.4 mm **(fig. 84)**
27] Metacarpals: R and L 2nd metacarpal; L 3rd metacarpal; R 4th metacarpal **(figs. 85-86)**
28] 4 first row phalanges **(fig. 87)**
29] 5 second row phalanges including a thumb **(figs. 87-88)**
30] Left acetabulum fragment with part of ischial tuberosity **(fig. 89)**
31] Right acetabulum fragment **(fig. 89)**
32] Right sacral ala with posterior spine of sacrum **(fig. 89)**
33] Fragment of femur distal condyle **(fig. 90)**
34] Fragment of fibula shaft **(fig. 90)**
35] Distal fibula **(fig. 91)**
36] Axis and several cervical bodies **(fig. 92)**
37] Upper and lower thoracic bodies **(fig. 93)**
38] 4th lumbar **(fig. 94)**
39] 5th lumbar, body ht = 25.6 mm **(fig. 95)**
40] Collection of ribs **(fig. 96)**

Pathology
Bilateral depressions on the inferior surface of the fifth lumbar vertebra, with osteophytes, were the result of work-related degeneration.

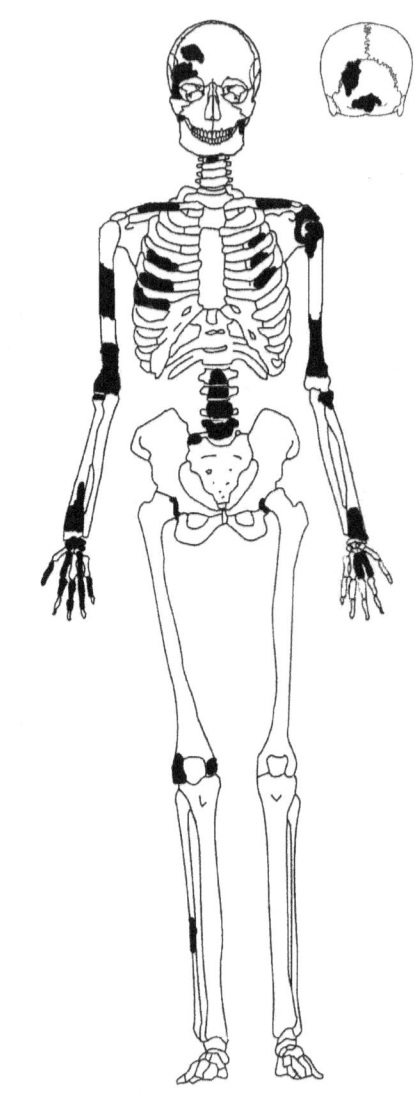

Fig. A. Adult skeleton: shaded areas preserved

Child

The child, which was probably not more than six or seven years old, is barely represented by only two skeletal parts. The first of these is a small lumbar vertebra centrum. It is apparent that the neural arches had already fused with the centrum, which means the child would have been between 3 to 7 years of age. The other is the crown of a partially formed, unerupted permanent molar tooth, the lower right first molar, which indicates the child was around six years of age.

Teeth:
41] Partially formed and unerupted lower RM1 **(fig. 97)**

Post Cranial Remains:
42] Child's lumbar vertebra centrum **(fig. 98)**

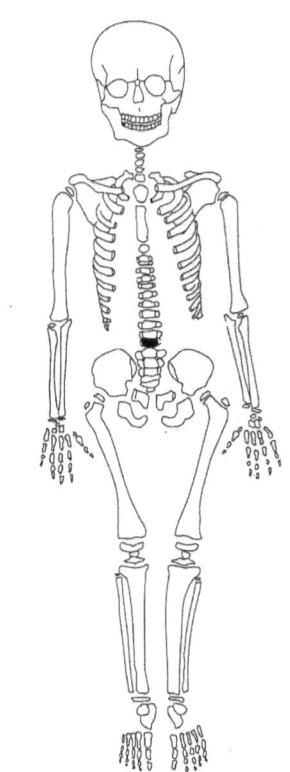

Fig. B. Child's skeleton: shaded areas preserved

Animal Remains
43] Sheep/goat premolar tooth **(fig. 100)**

Discussion and Conclusions

The surviving skeletal parts indicate that this is a double cremation, comprising remains from two individuals: an adult male of 25 years, much more fully represented than the second individual, a child, who but for the two fragments which survived to substantiate its existence would otherwise have been totally invisible in the archaeological record.

One reason for the apparent "incompleteness" of the skeletal remains in this cremation - the legs are barely represented - is that it was almost certainly disturbed. The top of the vase is missing and only the lower part of the vase survives. In addition, it is probable that those who collected the remains after the pyre was extinguished were not *very* meticulous but simply content to collect a few of the larger fragments to put in the burial urn. If they were the relatives of the deceased, they would naturally have had little enthusiasm for the sad task of gathering bones.

The Plakalona Tourloti cremation weighed 495g, and a scan of the shaded areas of the skeleton above **(fig. A)**, indicates that roughly 10% of the adult skeleton is preserved. The weights of two LMIIIC cremations from Pezoulos Atsipadhes, Rethymnon, are given as 1780g and 200g, respectively (Agelarakis, Kanta and Moody 2001, 78-80) At Lefkandi, in Euboea, where the earliest cremations date to the Submycenaean period[287], the majority of the cremations (46/52) weighed under 100 g., whereas the weights of thirteen Geometric cremations from Lower Gypsadhes, Knossos, were more substantial, ranging from 150g to 1650g with a mean of 613.85g ± 393.64g (Musgrave 1980, 443).[288] At Olynthus, 15 of the 53 cremations contained ashes and very few bones (Robinson 1942), while at Perati, not more than a third and often only a tiny amount of the skeleton was collected (Iakovides 1969-1970).

At Kavoussi, the Dark Age cremations had weights ranging from 18g to 2134g. Most of the burials were judged to be disturbed and weighed from as little as 18g to less than 1102g; half of these weighed under 487g and the rest weighed between 526 & 967g. The primary burials weighed between 1121.3g and 2134g. Some of the burials were comingled, i.e. they represented two and sometimes even three individuals (Liston 1993, 95 and 129).

It took several centuries before the rite of cremation replaced the custom of inhumation in Crete. There are nearly a dozen known sites in eastern Crete where early cremation burials dating to LMIIIC and possibly even as early as LMIIIA2/B at Olous (Kanta 2001), have been found **(Table 1)**. None has been the subject of anthropological study, with the exception of the Kritsas burials. Pyxis 172 contained a *cremated* adolescent (14-15 years old) with an *inhumed* adult, whose sex was undetermined. Pyxis 173 contained a double cremation, with one adult male aged 35-45 years

---

[287] Themelis 1980, 210.

[288] By way of comparison with the Lefkandi cremations, Musgrave (1980) quotes statistics for Romano-British cremations, which show that a substantial cremation might weigh as much as 2, 000g, yet weights of only 10g are quite frequent. J. S. Weiner (1951) observed that 72% of the cremations at Roman Dorchester weighed less than 800 g, while Calvin Wells (1960) noted that few of the Romano-British cremations he studied were more than 20% complete.

and a child of 5-8 years. The adult was represented by 550 fragments, but the weight of these cremated remains is not mentioned in the publication; while the child was represented by 15 fragments weighing only 7.2g (Tsipopoulou and Little 2001, 88).

The Plakalona cremation is particularly interesting because, like the Kritsas example, it shows that both adults and quite young children were accorded the same rites of cremation burial in LMIIIC. In the past, the presence of cremated children could easily have gone unrecognized due to the lack of anthropological studies and also due to the idea, which can be traced back to ancient sources, that children, or rather infants, were excluded from this form of burial rite. Pliny the Elder in *Naturalis Historia* 7:72, states that people were not cremated before the teething age. Speculation about the reasons for this and about the structure of society have concluded that children and particularly infants, having made a negligible contribution to society, were dispatched with little trouble or expenditure after death.[289]

The Plakalona child has a dental age of about six years, yet its cremation shows that this form of burial was not reserved exclusively for adults. At Olous, where both inhumation and cremation were practiced in LMIIIA2-B, three pithoi were reported to have contained the inhumed bones of 'infants'. However, on the one hand their age is not specified and on the other hand, mixed burial rites were practiced in the same cemetery. Mixed rites are seen at several LMIIIC sites (see **Table 1**) illustrating a constellation of behaviours. The great diversity of tomb types in another cemetery at Krya (built tholoi, pseudo tholoi, a square tholos with keel vault, chamber tomb, shaft grave and earth chasm), may reflect the diverse origins of that population, with elements from abroad[290], which could have been a conduit for the introduction of the custom of cremation which eventually took root.

In conclusion, were it not for two small fragments, the Plakalona child would have been all but lost. Whether or not infants (under a year old and without teeth) were indeed excluded from cremation burial should remain an open question until more cremation burials have come to light and are submitted to specialist scrutiny. Diversity in mortuary behaviour at this period seems to imply a liberal attitude and a tolerance towards individualistic expressions of beliefs which ushered in a new era of social cohesion.

P.J.P. McGeorge
tinamcgeorge@hotmail.co.uk

Acknowledgements

I express my warmest thanks to Ms Vili Apostolakou for facilitating the study in every way, to Mr Constantinos Paschalidis for his irrepressible enthusiasm and Mr Chronis Papanikolopoulos for outstanding photos.

---

[289] Garland 1985.
[290] Kanta and Davaras, 2004.

Table 1. EARLY CREMATION BURIALS IN EASTERN CRETE

SITE NAME	TOMB TYPES RECEPTACLES	NUMBER OF BURIALS	DATE	EXCAVATOR - PUBLICATIONS
Kritsa	Tholos Pyxis	Double cremation in extensive cemetery	LMIIIC	Platon 1953, 444-445; Davaras 1973, 162; Tsipopoulou and Little 2001, 83-96
Krya	Variety tholoi & Chamber tombs	Mainly inhumations with rare cremations	LMIIIC-PG	Davaras C. *ArchDelt* 27 (1972) B2, 645-654; Kanta and Davaras 2004.
Mesa Mouliana *Sellades*	Tholos Large Krater & Pyxis	Tomb A contained inhumations & cremations Part of unexcavated cemetery	LMIIIC late/Sub-Minoan	Xanthoudides 1904, 21-52; Davaras 1973, 163; Platon 1959, 389.
Myrsini	Chamber Tomb Urn	Cremation compared to Mouliana & Praisos	LMIIIC	Platon 1959a, 372-373, Davaras 1973, 162 and n. 48
Olous	25 Pithoi & 3 bath tubs inserted into rock cavities	Mixed rites: 26 inhumations; 25 pithos cremations included 3 inhumed children. Two double and one triple cremation in bath tubs	LMIIIC/ revised: LMIIIA2-B	Van Effenterre 1948; Davaras 1973, 163-164, Kanta 2001.
Praisos *Photoula*	Tholos Pyxis	Child cremation in pyxis found in larnax with inhumed young adult male.	LMIIIC	Platon 1960, 303-305, Davaras 1973, 162.
Tourloti *Plakatona*	Chamber Tomb Stamnos	Double cremation	LMIIIC early	Papadakis 1984, 306.
Vrokastro *Karakovilia*	Tholos & 5 bone enclosures, some with pyres Jars	5 adult cremations in large tholos with inhumed child.	Sub-Minoan/ PG	Davaras, 1973, 164.
Vrokastro *Kopranes*	Tholos and bone enclosures	One of the three tholoi & 6 bone enclosures had cremations	LMIII/PG	Davaras, 1973, 164.
Vrokastro *Mazichortia*	Tholos and bone enclosures	Cremation	PG/EG	Davaras, 1973, 164.
Zakro *Palaimylos*	Stirrup Jar & Pyxis	Cremation	LMIIIC/ Sub-Minoan	Davaras 1973, 158-161; Davaras 1973a, 585-596.

Summary (Περίληψη)

ΤΟ ΥΣΤΕΡΟΜΙΝΩΙΚΟ III ΝΕΚΡΟΤΑΦΕΙΟ ΤΗΣ ΤΟΥΡΛΩΤΗΣ ΣΗΤΕΙΑΣ.
Ο «ΖΩΓΡΑΦΟΣ ΤΟΥ ΞΑΝΘΟΥΔΙΔΗ» ΚΑΙ Ο ΠΟΛΥΠΟΔΙΚΟΣ ΡΥΘΜΟΣ ΣΤΗΝ ΑΝΑΤΟΛΙΚΗ ΚΡΗΤΗ.

Στην εργασία αυτή παρουσιάζονται τα αποτελέσματα της μελέτης δύο θαλαμωτών τάφων, καθώς και μιας ομάδας αγγείων από το ΥΜ III νεκροταφείο στη θέση Πλακάλωνα Τουρλωτής Σητείας, στην ανατολική Κρήτη. Η θέση του ΥΜ III νεκροταφείου, καθώς και του σύγχρονου χωριού της Τουρλωτής βρίσκεται στα υψώματα πίσω από το λιμάνι του Μόχλου και πάνω στο δρόμο από τον κόλπο του Μιραμπέλλου προς τον Πετρά και το Παλαίκαστρο.

Ο πρώτος θαλαμωτός τάφος ανεσκάφη από τη Μεταξία Τσιποπούλου το 1984. Περιείχε δύο παραμερισμένες ταφές και δύο αγγεία: ένα τρίωτο πιθαμφορέα και μια τριφυλλόστομη οινοχόη. Το πρώτο αγγείο, που ίσως να προέρχεται από την Κνωσό, χρονολογείται στην ΥΜ ΙΙΙΑ1 περίοδο και αντανακλά την εμπορική κυριαρχία της 'μυκηναϊκής πρωτεύουσας' της Κρήτης, πριν από την πτώση της. Η σύγχρονη, τριφυλλόστομη οινοχόη αποτελεί συνήθη τύπο του αποκαλούμενου 'κεραμικού εργαστηρίου των Μόχλου-Μυρσίνης-Τουρλωτής'. Στις οινοχόες του τύπου αυτού επιβιώνουν πολλά παραδοσιακά μορφολογικά και διακοσμητικά χαρακτηριστικά της προ-μυκηναϊκής μινωικής κεραμικής. Τέλος, παρουσιάζονται για πρώτη φορά τρεις παρόμοιες οινοχόες από το ίδιο εργαστήριο, που προέρχονται από λαθρανασκαφές και φυλάσσονται σήμερα στο Εθνικό Αρχαιολογικό Μουσείο.

Ο δεύτερος θαλαμωτός τάφος ανεσκάφη από το Νικόλαο Παπαδάκη το ίδιο έτος. Περιείχε έξι αγγεία, δύο σφονδύλια και μία χάνδρα, καθώς και τα καμμένα οστά ενός νέου άνδρα και ενός παιδιού, που χρονολογούνται στην πρώιμη ΥΜ ΙΙΙΓ περίοδο. Από τους τέσσερις ψευδόστομους αμφορείς του συνόλου ο ένας διακοσμείται κατά τον πολυποδικό ρυθμό, ο δεύτερος φέρει εικονιστική παράσταση θαλάσσιου τοπίου και οι δύο τελευταίοι πρέπει να προέρχονται από τη βόρεια Ρόδο. Το σύνολο συμπληρώνει ο στάμνος, που περιείχε τα καμμένα οστά και το πώμα του. Η ανεύρεση των λειψάνων ανδρός και παιδιού στο ίδιο τεφροδόχο αγγείο, εύρημα που απαντά σε δύο ακόμη σύγχρονα παραδείγματα στο γειτονικό νεκροταφείο της Κριτσάς, ίσως να μαρτυρεί ένα συγκεκριμένο ταφικό έθιμο ή ένα άγνωστο ιστορικό γεγονός σε αυτήν την περιοχή.

Το τρίτο σύνολο ευρημάτων από το νεκροταφείο της Τουρλωτής παραδόθηκε από το Μανώλη Φυγετάκη στο Μουσείο Σητείας πριν από πενήντα χρόνια. Περιλαμβάνει δύο πρόχους, έναν πιεσμένου σχήματος ψευδόστομο αμφορέα του 'εργαστηρίου του Παλαικάστρου', δύο ψευδόστομους αμφορείς του πυκνού πολυποδικού ρυθμού και έναν τελευταίο, που πρέπει να προέρχεται από τη Σκύρο. Τα αγγεία αυτά χρονολογούνται μεταξύ της πρώιμης και της μέσης ΥΜ ΙΙΙΓ περιόδου.

Η παρουσίαση των παραπάνω ευρημάτων από το νεκροταφείο διαμορφώνει έμμεσα ένα μέρος της εικόνας της ζωής στην Τουρλωτή και του δικτύου των σχέσεών των ανθρώπων της, αρχικά με τη μυκηναϊκή Κνωσό και κατόπιν με την ηπειρωτική χώρα, τη Σκύρο και τα Δωδεκάνησα κατά τη μετανακτορική περίοδο. Το εύρημα της κοινής ταφικής πυράς των δύο νεκρών προσφέρει νέα στοιχεία για τις ταφικές πρακτικές στην ανατολική Κρήτη και νέα ερωτήματα.

Στο δεύτερο μέρος της εργασίας παρουσιάζεται ο ψευδόστομος αμφορέας του πολυποδικού πυκνού ρυθμού ΜΣ 4026 από την παράδοση Φυγετάκη, ο οποίος αποδίδεται σε έναν συγκεκριμένο και διακριτό κεραμέα, που αποκαλείται συμβατικά «Ζωγράφος του Ξανθουδίδη». Στον καλλιτέχνη αυτόν αποδίδονται δύο ακόμη γνωστοί ψευδόστομοι αμφορείς από παλαιές ανασκαφές στα Μουλιανά, καθώς και ένας ακόμη, που φυλάσσεται σήμερα στο Μουσείο Κυκλαδικής Τέχνης (Ίδρυμα Ν.Π. Γουλανδρή). Αναλύεται η κοινή τεχνοτροπία των τεσσάρων αγγείων και τα προσωπικά καλλιτεχνικά ιδιώματα του «Ζωγράφου του Ξανθουδίδη» Ακόμη ανιχνεύεται η καλλιτεχνική συγγένεια του «Ζωγράφου» με αγγεία και λάρνακες άλλων εργαστηρίων της ανατολικής Κρήτης. Στη συνέχεια γίνεται συζήτηση για το ζήτημα της χρονολόγησης του πολυποδικού πυκνού ρυθμού και τέλος εντοπίζονται τα κοινά χαρακτηριστικά των αγγείων του ρυθμού αυτού από την ανατολική Κρήτη και η διασπορά τους στο υπόλοιπο Αιγαίο.

Στο τελευταίο μέρος παρουσιάζεται αναλυτικά η ανθρωπολογική μελέτη τού σκελετικού υλικού, που προέρχεται από την κοινή πυρά των δύο νεκρών του τάφου, που ανέσκαψε ο Νικόλαος Παπαδάκης. Αποδεικνύεται ότι το υλικό ανήκει σε δύο άτομα, έναν ενήλικα 25 ετών με παθολογικά ευρήματα στη σπονδυλική στήλη, κι ένα παιδί 6 ετών. Η εύρεση του παιδιού αποδεικνύει ότι δικαίωμα στην πυρά δεν είχαν μόνον οι ενήλικες, αλλά και τα παιδιά. Η πρώιμη αυτή περίπτωση είναι μοναδική μέχρι τώρα στο νεκροταφείο τής Τουρλωτής, όπου επικρατούσε ο ενταφιασμός. Η μεικτή πρακτική πυράς και ενταφιασμού στην Ανατολική Κρήτη κράτησε μερικούς αιώνες. Το γεγονός αυτό και η έλλειψη ανθρωπολογικών μελετών των καύσεων θέτει σε αμφισβήτηση τη θεωρία του αποκλεισμού των παιδιών από την πυρά.

Summary (Estratto)

LA NECROPOLI TARDO-MINOICA III DI TOURLOTÌ (SITIA).
IL «PITTORE DI XANTHOUDIDIS» E L' *OCTOPUS STYLE* NELLA CRETA ORIENTALE.

In questo lavoro sono presentati i risultati dello studio di due tombe a camera e di un gruppo di vasi provenienti dalla necropoli TM III individuata in contrada Plakalona Tourlotì (Sitia), nella Creta orientale. La posizione della necropoli TM III così come del moderno villaggio di Tourlotì si trova sulle colline dietro il porto di Mochlos, sulla strada che va dalla Baia di Mirabello fino a Petra ed a Palekastro.

La prima tomba a camera è stata scavata da Metaxia Tsipopoulou nel 1984. Essa conteneva due sepolture dismesse e due vasi: un'anfora piriforme triansata e un'oinochoè trilobata. Il primo vaso, proveniente forse da Knossos, è datato al TM IIIA1 e riflette la posizione commerciale dominante della "capitale micenea" di Creta, prima della caduta. L'oinochoè trilobata, ad esso contemporaneo, risulta essere un tipo comune della cosiddetta "officina ceramica di Mochlos-Myrsini-Tourlotì". Nelle oinochoè di questo tipo sopravvivono molte caratteristiche tradizionali morfologiche e decorative della ceramica minoica pre-micenea. Infine, sono presentate per la prima volta tre oinochoè simili dallo stesso laboratorio, provenienti da scavi clandestini ed oggi conservate presso il Museo Archeologico Nazionale di Atene.

La seconda tomba a camera è stata scavata da Nikos Papadakis, nello stesso anno (1984). Essa conteneva sei vasi, due fuseruole e un pendente di faïence, e ossa bruciate appartenenti ad un giovane uomo e un bambino, risalente agli inizi del TM IIIC. Delle quattro anfore a staffa, una è decorata con l' *Octopus Style*, la seconda reca immagini di un paesaggio marino e le ultime due dovrebbero provenire dalla zona nord dell'isola di Rodi. Il gruppo è completato da uno stamnos, che conteneva le ossa bruciate, e dal suo coperchio. La scoperta di resti di un adulto e di un ragazzo nella stessa urna cineraria, fatto che si ritrova in altri due esempi contemporanei nella vicina necropoli di Kritsà, testimonia forse un determinato uso funerario o uno sconosciuto avvenimento storico in questa regione.

Il terzo gruppo di reperti provenienti dalla necropoli di Tourlotì, è stato consegnato da Manolis Fygetakis presso il Museo di Sitia cinquant'anni fa. Esso comprende due brocche, un'anfora a staffa di forma schiacciata dell' "officina di Palekastro", due anfore a staffa dello stile denso del polpo e un'ultima, che deve provenire da Skyros. Queste ceramiche sono datate tra l'inizio e la metà del TM IIIC.

La presentazione di questi risultati dalla necropoli crea indirettamente un'immagine parziale della vita a Tourlotì e la rete di relazioni dei suoi abitanti dapprima con la Knossos micenea e poi con la terraferma, Skyros e con il Dodecanneso durante il periodo post-palaziale. Il rinvenimento della pira funebre comune a due defunti offre nuove informazioni sulle pratiche di sepoltura nella Creta orientale, e fa sorgere nuovi interrogativi.

Nella seconda parte del lavoro è presentata l'anfora a staffa dello *Close Octopus Style*, (n. Inv. MS 4026) consegnata da Fygetakis, che è attribuita ad uno specifico e distinto ceramista, chiamato convenzionalmente «Pittore di Xanthoudidis». A questo artista sono attribuite altre due note anfore a staffa rinvenute nei vecchi scavi a Moulianà, e una terza che è oggi conservata presso il Museo di Arte Cicladica (Fondazione N.P. Goulandrì) ad Atene.

È analizzata la tecnica comune ai quattro vasi ed il personale stile artistico del «Pittore di Xanthoudidis». Si rintraccia inoltre l'affinità artistica del «Pittore» in vasi e "larnakes" di altri laboratori della Creta orientale. Segue quindi un dibattito sulla questione della cronologia dello *Close Octopus Style* ed, infine, si localizzano le caratteristiche comuni dei vasi di questo stile nella Creta orientale e la loro diffusione nel Mar Egeo.

Nell' ultima parte del libro è presentato analiticamente lo studio dei materiali antropologici, dalla pira comune dei due defunti della tomba, che è stata scavata da Nikos Papadakis. Risulta che il materiale appartiene a due individui, un maggiorenne di 25 anni, con evidenze patologiche sulla colonna verterbrale, e un bambino di 6 anni, la cui scoperta dimostra che il diritto alla cremazione era riservato pure ai minorenni. Questo caso, datato all'inizio del TMIIIC, è finora unico nei confronti del cimitero di Tourloti, dove prevaleva la sepoltura. La pratica mista tra cremazione e sepoltura alla Creta orientale durò alcuni secoli. Questo fatto, accostato alla mancanza di studi antropologici sulla cremazione, mette in dubbio la teoria dell'esclusione dei bambini dalla creamazione.

Abbreviations

ANM: Agios Nikolaos Archaeological Museum
BE: Registration number
HM: Herakleion Archaeological Museum
FM: Furumark motif
FS: Furumark shape
MCA: Museum of Cycladic Art, N.P. Goulandris Foundation
NAM: National Archaeological Museum
NM: Naxos Archaeological Museum
P: INSTAPEC
PM: Patras Archaeological Museum
SM: Siteia Archaeological Museum

The bibliographical abbreviations used follow the standards outlined in the American Journal of Archaeology 95 (1991), 4-16.

Bibliography

Aggelarakis, Kanta and Moody 2001: Aggelarakis A., Kanta A., Moody J., "Cremation Burial in LM IIIC – Sub Minoan Crete and the Cemetery at Pezoulos Atsipades, Crete", in Stampolidis N.C. (ed.), *Proceedings of the Symposium: Crematios in the Bronze and the Early Iron Age. Rhodes, 29 April – 2 May 1999*, Athens 2001, 69-82.

Alberti and Doi: Alberti L., Doi M., "Una Giara a Staffa del Museo Goulandris", *SMEA* 41 (1999), 5-15.

Alexiou 1954: Alexiou S., "Υστερομινωικός Τάφος Παχυάμμου", *CretChron* 8 (1954), 399-412.

Alexiou 1967: Alexiou S., *Υστερομινωικοί Τάφοι Λιμένος Κνωσού (Κατσαμπά)*, Athens 1967.

Alexiou and Davaras 1964: Alexiou S., Davaras K., "Αρχαιότητες και Μνημεία Κρήτης", *ArchDelt* 19 (1964) B3, 436-447.

Andersson (forthcoming): Andersson E., Mårtensson L., Nosch M.L., "Textile Production in the Late Bronze Age Khania", in *10th International Cretological Congress, Khania, 1-8 October 2006*, (poster presentation).

Andreadaki-Vlazaki and Papadopoulou 2005: Andreadaki-Vlazaki M., Papadopoulou E., "The Habitation at Khamalevri, Rethymnon, during the 12th Century BC", in D'Agata A.L., Moody J., Williams E. (eds.), *Ariadne's Threads. Connections between Crete and the Greek Mainland in Late Minoan III (LM IIIA2 to LM IIIC), Proceedings of the International Workshop held at Athens, Scuola Archeologica Italiana, 5-6 April 2003*, Atene 2005, 353-397.

Apostolakou 1998: Apostolakou V., "Υστερομινωικοί ΙΙΙ Τάφοι στη Γρα Λυγιά Ιεράπετρας", *ArchDelt* 53 (1998) A, 25-88, pls.5-24.

Banou 2005: Banou E., "LM III Mokhlos (East Crete) versus LM III Viannos (Central Eastern Crete): Differences and Similarities", in D'Agata A.L., Moody J., Williams E. (eds.), *Ariadne's Threads. Connections between Crete and the Greek Mainland in Late Minoan III (LM IIIA2 to LM IIIC), Proceedings of the International Workshop held at Athens, Scuola Archeologica Italiana, 5-6 April 2003*, Atene 2005, 145-173.

Banou and Rethemiotakis 1997: Banou E., Rethemiotakis G., "Centre and Periphery: New Evidence for the Relations between Knossos and the Area of Viannos in the LM II-IIIA Periods", in Driessen J., Farnoux A. (eds.), *La Crète Mycénienne, Actes de la Tâble Rônde Internationale, Organisée par l' École Française d' Athènes, 26-28 Mars 1991* (BCH suppl.30), Athènes 1997, 23-57.

Barber 1991: Barber E.J.W., *Prehistoric Textiles*, Princeton 1991.

Benzi 1975: Benzi M., *Ceramica Micenea in Attica*, Milano 1975.

Benzi 1992: Benzi M., *Rodi e la Civiltà Micenea*, vols. I-II, Roma 1992.

Betancourt 1983: Betancourt P.P., *The Cretan Collection in the University Museum, University of Pennsylvania, vol.I: Minoan Objects Excavated from Vasilike, Pseira, Sphoungaras, Priniatikos Pyrgos, and Other Sites*, (University Museum Monographs 47), Pennsylvania 1983.

Betancourt 1985: Betancourt P.P., *The History of Minoan Pottery*, Princeton 1985.

Blegen 1937: Blegen C.W., *Prosymna. The Helladic Settlement Preceding the Argive Heraeum*, I-II, Cambridge 1937.

Blegen et al. 1973: Blegen C.W., Rawson M., Lord Taylour W., Donovan W.P., *The Palace of Nestor at Pylos in Western Messenia, vol. III, Acropolis and Lower Town Tholoi, Grave Circle, and Discoveries outside the Citadel*, Princeton 1973.

Borgna 2003: Borgna E., *Il Complesso di Ceramica Tardominoico III dell' Acropoli Mediana di Festos*, (Studi di Archeologia Cretese III), Padova 2003.

Bosanquet and Dawkins 1923: Bosanquet R.C., Dawkins R.M., *The Unpublished Objects from the Palaikastro Excavations, 1902-1906*, (BSA suppl.1) London 1923.

Buchholz 1959: Buchholz H.G., *Zur Herkunft der Kretischen Doppelaxt. Geschichte und Auswärtige Beziehungen Eines Minoischen Kultsymbols*, München 1959.

Cavanagh and Mee 1998: Cavanagh W., Mee C., *A Private Place: Death in Prehistoric Greece*, (SIMA CXXV), Jonsered 1998.

Coulson 1997: Coulson W.D.E., "The Late Minoan IIIC Period on the Kastro at Kavousi", in Driessen J., Farnoux A. (eds.), *La Crète Mycénienne, Actes de la Table Rônde Internationale, Organisée par l' École Française d' Athènes, 26-28 Mars 1991* (BCH suppl.30), Athènes 1997, 59-72.

D'Agata 1999: D'Agata A.L., "Defining a Pattern of Continuity during the Dark Age in Central-Western Crete: Ceramic Evidence from the Settlement of Thronos/Kefala (Ancient Sybrita)", *SMEA* 41 (1999), 181-218.

D'Agata 2007: D'Agata A.L., "Evolutionary Paradigms and Late Minoan III. On a Definition of LM IIIC Middle", in Deger-Jalkotzy S., Zavadil M. (eds.), *LH III C Chronology and Synchronisms II. LH III C Middle, Proceedings of the International Workshop Held at the Austrian Academy of Sciences at Vienna, October 29th and 30th, 2004*, Wien 2007, 89-118.

Daux 1960: Daux G., "Chronique des Fouilles 1959", *BCH* 84 (1960), 617-868.

Davaras 1973: Davaras C., "Cremations in Minoan and Sub-Minoan Crete", in *Antichità Cretesi, Studi in Onore di Doro Levi*, I (Cronache di Archeologia 12), Catania 1973, 158-167, pl.28.

Davaras 1973a: Davaras C., "Αρχαιότητες και Μνημεία της Ανατολικής Κρήτης", *ArchDelt* 28 (1973) B2, 585-596.

Davaras 1986: Davaras C., "Une Tombe à Voûte en Crète Orientale", in Nicolet C. (ed.), *Aux Origines de l' Hellénisme. La Crète et la Grèce. Hommage à Henri Van Effenterre*, Paris 1986, 297-310.

Demakopoulou 1997: Demakopoulou K., "Crete and the Argolid in the LM II/LH IIB to IIIA1 Periods. Evidence from Kokla", in Driessen J., Farnoux A. (eds.), *La Crète Mycénienne, Actes de la Table Rônde Internationale, Organisée par l' École Française d' Athènes, 26-28 Mars 1991* (BCH suppl.30), Athènes 1997, 101-112.

Desborough 1964: Desborough V.R. d'A., *The Last Mycenaeans and Their Successors*, Oxford[2] 1966.

Deshayes 1960: Deshayes J., *Les Outils de Bronze, de l' Indus au Danube (IVe au IIe Millénaire)*, vols. I-II, Paris 1960.

Detorakis 1990: Detorakis T., *Στέφανος Ξανθουδίδης. Βιογραφικά – Βιβλιογραφικά*, Herakleion 1990.

De Wild 2001: de Wild D., "Textile Remains on Vases from Tomb 1 and Tomb 2C", in Karantzali E., *The Mycenaean Cemetery at Pylona on Rhodes*, (BAR Int.Series 988) Oxford 2001, 114-116.

Dickinson 2006: Dickinson O., *The Aegean from Bronze Age to Iron Age, Continuity and Change between the twelfth and eighth Centuries BC*, London and New York 2006.

Dimopoulou and Rethemiotakis 1978: Dimopoulou-Rethemiotaki N., Rethemiotakis G., "Υστερομινωικό Νεκροταφείο στο Μετόχι Καλού Ηρακλείου", *ArchDelt* 33 (1978) A, 40-109, pls.16-22.

Doumas and Marangou 1978: Doumas C., Marangou L., *Exhibition of Ancient Greek Art from the N.P. Goulandris Collection*, Athens 1978.

Effinger 1996: Effinger M., *Minoischer Schmuck*, (BAR Int.Series 646), Oxford 1996.

Evans 1906: Evans A.J., *The Prehistoric Tombs of Knossos. I. The Cemetery of Zafer Papoura, II. The Royal Tomb of Isopata*, London 1906.

Evans 1914: Evans A., *The Tomb of the Double Axes and Associated Group and Pillar Rooms and Ritual Vessels of the 'Little Palace' at Knossos*, London 1914.

French 1992: French E.B., "Archaeology in Greece 1991-1992", *AR* 38 (1991-1992), 3-70.

Furumark 1941: Furumark A., *The Mycenaean Pottery, Analysis and Classification*, Stockholm 1941.

Garland 1985: Garland R., *The Greek Way of Death*, Ithaca NY, Cornell University Press, 1985.

Georgiadis 1940: Georgiadis M. (ed.), *Μνημόσυνα Στεφ. Ξανθουδίδου, Ιωσήφ Χατζηδάκη, 1938-1940*, Herakleion 1940.

Grammatikaki 1998: Grammatikaki E., "Χάλκινη Ημισφαιρική Φιάλη με Υπολείματα Υφάσματος", in Stampolidis N.C., Karetsou A. (eds.), *East Mediterrannean. Cyprus – Dodecanese – Crete, 16th-6th century BC*, (Exhibition Catalogue) Herakleion 1998, 239.

Hallager 1993: Hallager B.P., "Mycenaean Pottery in Crete", in Zerner C., Zerner P. and Winder J. (eds.), *Proceedings of the International Conference: WACE AND BLEGEN, Pottery as Evidence for Trade in the Aegean Bronze Age 1939-1989. Athens, December 2-3, 1989*, Amsterdam 1993, 263-269.

Hallager and Hallager 2000: Hallager E., Hallager B.P. (eds.), *The Greek-Swedish Excavations at the Agia Aikaterini Square Kastelli, Khania 1970-1987. vol.II, The Late Minoan IIIC Settlement*, Stockholm 2000.

Hallager and Hallager 2003: Hallager E., Hallager B.P. (eds.), *The Greek-Swedish Excavations at the Agia Aikaterini Square Kastelli, Khania 1970-1987 and 2001. vols.III:1 and III:2, The Late Minoan IIIB:2 Settlement*, Stockholm 2003,

Hallager and McGeorge 1992: Hallager B.P., McGeorge P.J.P., *Late Minoan III Burials at Khania*, (SIMA XCIII), Göteborg 1992.

Hatzaki 2005: Hatzaki E.M., *Knossos. The Little Palace*, (BSA suppl.38) Oxford and Northampton 2005.

Hatzaki 2007: Hatzaki E., "Final Palatial (LM II-LM IIIA2) and Postpalatial (LM IIIB-LM IIIC Early): The MUM South Sector, Long Corridor Cists, MUM Pits (8, 10-11), Makritikhos 'Kitchen', MUM North Platform Pits and SEX Southern Half Groups", in Momigliano N. (ed.), *Knossos Pottery Handbook. Neolithic and Bronze Age (Minoan)*, (BSA studies 14) London 2007, 197-251.

Hatzaki 2007a: Hatzaki E., "Well 576: The Pottery Deposits and Ceramic Sequence", in MacGillivray J.A., Sackett L.H. and Driessen J.M. (eds.), *Palaikastro: Two Late Minoan Wells*, (BSA suppl. 43), London 2007, 15-94.

Höckmann 1980: Höckmann O., "Lanze und Speer im Spätminoischen und Mykenischen Griechenland", *JRGZM* 27 (1980), 13-158, pls.1-6.

Hood and de Jong 1952: Hood M.S.F., de Jong P., "Late Minoan Warrior-Graves from Ayios Ioannis and the New Hospital Site in Knossos", *BSA* 47 (1952), 243-277.

Hood, Huxley and Sandars 1958-1959: Hood S., Huxley G., Sandars N., "A Minoan Cemetery on Upper Gypsades", *BSA* 53-54 (1958-1959), 194-262, pls.49-63.

Iakovidis 1969-1970: Iakovidis S., *Περατή. Το Νεκροταφείον*, vols. Α-Γ, Athens 1969-1970.

Iakovidis 1977: Iakovidis S., "On the Use of Mycenaean 'Buttons'", *BSA* 72 (1977), 113-119, pls. 24-25.

Kanta 1980: Kanta A., *The Late Minoan III Period in Crete. A Survey of Sites, Pottery and Their Distribution*, (SIMA 58) Göteborg 1980.

Kanta 2001: Kanta A., "The Cremations of Olous and the Custom of Cremation in Bronze Age Crete", in Stampolidis N.C. (ed.), *Proceedings of the Symposium: Crematios in the Bronze and the Early Iron Age. Rhodes, 29 April – 2 May1999*, Athens 2001, 59-68.

Kanta 2003: Kanta A., "Aristocrats – Traiders – Emigrants – Settlers. Crete in the Closing Phases of the Bronze Age", in Stampolidis N.C., Karageorghis V. (eds.), *SEA ROUTES...*

Interconnections in the Mediterranean 16ᵗʰ – 6ᵗʰ c.B.C., Proceedings of the International Symposium held at Rethymnon, Crete, September 29ᵗʰ – October 2ⁿᵈ 2002, Athens 2003, 173-186.

Kanta and Davaras 2004: Kanta A., Davaras C., "The Cemetery of Krya, District of Sitia. Developments at the End of the LBA and the Beginning of the EIA in East Crete", in Stampolidis N.C., Yiannikouri A. (eds.), *Aegean in the Early Iron Age. Proceedings of the International Symposium,* Athens 2004, 149-156.

Karantzali 1986: Karantzali E., "Une Tombe du Minoen Récent III B à la Canée", *BCH* 110 (1986), 53-87.

Karantzali 1998: Karantzali E., "Ψευδόστομος Αμφορέας", in Stampolidis N.C., Karetsou A. (eds.), *East Mediterrannean. Cyprus – Dodecanese – Crete, 16ᵗʰ-6ᵗʰ century BC,* (Exhibition Catalogue) Herakleion 1998, 66-67.

Karantzali 2001: Karantzali E., *The Mycenaean Cemetery at Pylona on Rhodes,* (BAR Int.Series 988), Oxford 2001.

Kardara 1977: Kardara C., *Απλώματα Νάξου, Κινητά Ευρήματα Τάφων Α και Β,* Athens 1977.

Kavvadias 1912: Kavvadias P., 'Περί των εν Κεφαλληνία Ανασκαφών', *Prakt* 1912, 247-268.

Konstantinidi 2001: Konstantinidi E., *Jewellery Revealed in the Burial Contexts of the Greek Bronze Age,* (BAR Int. Series 912), Oxford 2001.

Kopaka 2002: Kopaka K., "Στέφανος Ξανθουδίδης. Ο Πρωτεργάτης της Κρητικής Αρχαιολογίας", (Studies in honour of R.F. Willets), *Cretan Studies* 7 (2002), 125-140.

Leekley and Noyes 1975: Leekley D., Noyes R., *Archaeological Excavations in the Greek Islands,* New Jersey 1975.

Liston 1993: Liston M.A., *The Human Skeletal Remains from Kavoussi, Crete: A Bioarchaeological Analysis,* (unpublished D. Phil, University of Tennessee, 1993).

Löwe 1996: Löwe W., *Spätbronzezeitliche Bestattungen auf Kreta,* (BAR Int.Series 642), Oxford 1996.

Macdonald 1985: Macdonald C.F., *The Relationship of Crete and Mainland Greece to the Islands of the South Aegean during the Late Bronze Age,* (unpublished D. Phil), Oxford 1985, vols. I-II.

Macdonald 1986: Macdonald C., "Problems of the Twelfth Century BC in the Dodecanese", *BSA* 81 (1986), 125-151.

MacGillivray 1997: MacGillivray J.A., "Late Minoan II and III Pottery and Chronology at Palaikastro: an Introduction", in Hallager E., Hallager B.P. (eds.), *Late Minoan Pottery Chronology and Terminology, Acts of a Meeting held at the Danish Institute at Athens, August 12-14, 1994,* Athens 1997, 193-207.

MacGillivray 1997a: MacGillivray J.A., "The Re-occupation of Eastern Crete in the Late Minoan II-IIIA1/2 Periods", in Driessen J., Farnoux A. (eds.), *La Crète Mycénienne, Actes de la Table Rônde Internationale, Organisée par l' École Française d' Athènes, 26-28 Mars 1991* (BCH suppl.30), Athènes 1997, 275-279.

MacGillivray, Sackett and Driessen 2007: MacGillivray J.A., Sackett L.H. and Driessen J.M. (eds.), *Palaikastro: Two Late Minoan Wells,* (BSA suppl. 43), London 2007.

Maran 2006: Maran J., "Coming to Terms with the Past: Ideology and Power in Late Helladic IIIC", in Deger-Jalkotzy S., Lemos I.S., (eds.), *Ancient Greece: From the Mycenaean Palaces to the Age of Homer,* Edinburgh 2006, 123-150.

Marangou 1996: Marangou L.I., *Αρχαία Κυκλαδική Τέχνη. Συλλογή Ν.Π. Γουλανδρή,* Athens 1996.

Matz 1951: Matz F., *Forschungen auf Kreta 1942,* Berlin 1951.

Mauri 1923-1924: Mauri A., "Jalissos – Scavi della Missione Archeologica Italiana a Rodi. Parte I", *ASAtene* 6-7 (1923-1924), 83-256.

Mavroeidis 1938: Mavroeidis M., "Μινωικά Ευρήματα (αρχαιολογικές έρευνες Σητείας)", *Driros* 8 (1938), 217-219.

Melas 1984: Melas E.M., "The Origins of Aegean Cremation", *Anthropologika* 5 (1984), 21-36.

Melas 1985: Melas E.M., *The Islands of Karpathos, Saros and Kasos in the Neolithic and Bronze Age,* (SIMA LXVIII) Göteborg 1985.

Melas 2001: Melas M., "Καύσεις Νεκρών – Προς Μια Αρχαιολογία του Φόβου", in Stampolidis N.C. (ed.), *Proceedings of the Symposium: Crematios in the Bronze and the Early Iron Age. Rhodes, 29 April – 2 May1999,* Athens 2001, 15-29.

Merousis 2000: Merousis N.I., *Οι Εικονογραφικοί Κύκλοι των ΥΜ ΙΙΙ Λαρνάκων. Οι Διαστάσεις της Εικονογραφίας στα Πλαίσια των Ταφικών Πρακτικών,* Thessaloniki 2000.

Montelius 1924: Montelius O., *La Grèce Préclassique,* Stockholm 1924.

Mook and Coulson 1997: Mook M.S., Coulson W.D.E., "Late Minoan IIIC Pottery from the Kastro at Kavousi", in Hallager E., Hallager B.P. (eds.), *Late Minoan Pottery Chronology and Terminology, Acts of a Meeting held at the Danish Institute at Athens, August 12-14, 1994,* Athens 1997, 337-370.

Moore and Taylour 1999: Moore A.D., Taylour W.D., *Well Built Mycenae. The Helleno-British Excavations within the Citadel at Mycenae, 1959-1969, (Fascicule 10) The Temple Complex,* Oxford 1999.

Morricone 1965-1966: Morricone L., "Eleona e Langada: Sepolcreti della Tarda Età del Bronzo a Coo", *ASAtene* 43-44 (1965-1966), 5-311.

Morris 1995: Morris C., "Fishy Tales from Knossos: a Minoan Larnax and Vase-Painter", in Morris C. (ed.), *Klados. Essays in Honour of J.N. Coldstream,* London 1995, 185-193.

Mosso 1907: Mosso A., *Escursioni nel Mediterraneo e gli Scavi di Creta,* Milano 1907.

Mosso 1910: Mosso A., *The Dawn of Mediterranean Civilisation,* London 1910.

Mountjoy 1993: Mountjoy P.A., *Mycenaean Pottery. An Introduction,* Oxford 1993.

Mountjoy 1994: Mountjoy P.A., *Μυκηναϊκή Γραπτή Κεραμική. Οδηγός Ταύτισης,* (Greek translation by Gontika D.), Αθήνα 1994.

Mountjoy 1995: Mountjoy P.A., *Mycenaean Athens,* (SIMA pocket-book 127), Jonsered 1995.

Mountjoy 1999: Mountjoy P.A., *Regional Mycenaean Decorated Pottery,* vols. I-II, Rahden/Westf. 1999.

Mountjoy 2003: Mountjoy P.A., *Knossos. The South House,* (BSA suppl.34) Oxford and Northampton 2003.

Musgrave 1980: Musgrave J.H.S., "The Human Remains from the Cemeteries", in Popham M.R., Sackett L.H., Themelis P.G. (eds.), *Lefkandi I, the Iron Age,* (BSA suppl.11) London 1980, 429-445.

Mylonas 1972-1973: Mylonas G.E., *Ο Ταφικός Κύκλος Β των Μυκηνών,* vols. I-II, Athens 1972-1973.

Nezeri 2006: Nezeri P., "Ένα Υστερομινωικό Τοπικό «Εργαστήρι» Κεραμικής στην Επαρχία Ρεθύμνης", in Detorakis T., Kalokairinos A. (eds.), *Proceedings of the 9th International Cretological Congress, Elounda, 1-6 October 2001,* vol. A1 Prehistoric Period, Ηράκλειο 2006, 11-24.

Nicgorski 1999: Nicgorski A.M., "Polypus and the Poppy: Two Unusual Rhyta from the Mycenaean Cemetery at Mochlos", in Betancourt P.P., Karageorghis V., Lafineur R., Niemeier W.D. (eds.), *MELETEMATA Studies in Aegean Archaeology Presented to Malcom H. Wiener as He Enters His 65th Year,* (Aegaeum 20), Liège 1999, 537-542, pls.115-116.

Nightingale 2003: Nightingale G., "Glass and Faience Beads from Elateia-Alonaki Reflecting the Relationship between Centre and Periphery", in Kyparissi-Apostolika N., Papakonstantinou M. (eds.), *The Periphery of the Mycenaean World, Proceedings of the 2nd International Interdisciplinary Colloquium, Lamia, 26-30 September 1999,* Athens 2003, 311-319.

Nightingale 2004: Nightingale G., "Mykenisches Glas", in Kyriatsoulis A. (ed.), *Althellenische Technologie und Technik von der Prähistorischen bis zur Hellenistischen Zeit mit Schwerpunkt auf der Prähistorischen Epoche* (Proceedings of the International Conference), Ohlstadt 12-13 March 2003, Weilheim 2004, 171-194.

Nightingale 2007: Nightingale G., "Lefkandi. An Important Node in the International Exchange Network of Jewellery and Personal Adornment", in Galanaki I., Tomas H., Galanakis Y. Laffineur R. (eds), *Between the Aegean and Baltic Seas,*

Prehistory across the Borders, University of Zagreb, 11-14 April 2005, Zagreb, Mimara Museum, (Aegaeum 27), Liège 2007, 421-429, pl.106.

Nowicki 1990: Nowicki K., "The West Siteia Mountains at the Turn of the Bronze and Iron Ages", in Laffineur R. (ed.), *Aegaeum* 6 (1990), 161-182, pls.29-46.

Nowicki 2000: Nowicki K., *Defensible Sites in Crete c. 1200-800 B.C. (LM IIIB/IIIC through Early Geometric), (Aegaeum 21)*, Liège 2000.

Oikonomos 1928: Oikonomos G.P., "Γενική Έκθεσις του Γραμματέως", *Prakt* 1928, 1-33.

Oikonomos 1928a: Oikonomos G.P., "Αναμνηστικός Λόγος περί του Στεφάνου Ξανθουδίδου", *PraktAkAth* 3(1928), 628-634.

Paidoussis and Sbarounis 1975: Paidoussis M., Sbarounis C.N., "A Study of Cremated Bones from the Cemetery of Perati", *OpAth* 11 (1975), 129-160.

Panagiotaki 2000: Panagiotaki M., "Crete and Egypt: Contacts and Relationships Seen through Vitreous Materials", in Karetsou A (ed.), *Crete-Egypt, Three Thousand Years of Cultural Links*, (vol. II: studies), Athens 2000, 154-161.

Panagiotaki 2002: Panagiotaki M., "Φαγεντιανή – Κύανος – Ύαλος: Ύλες των Βασιλέων, των Θεών και των Νεκρών της Αρχαιότητας", in Kordas G., Antonaras A. (ed.), *Ιστορία και Τεχνολογία Αρχαίου Γυαλιού*, Athens 2002, 33-62.

Papadakis 1983 Papadakis N., *Sitia. Fatherland of Myson and Kornaros. A Historical, Archaeological and Cultural Guide*, Sitia 1983.

Papadakis 1984: Papadakis N., "Τουρλωτή Σητείας", *ArchDelt* 39 (1984) Β', 306.

Papadopoulos 1978-1979: Papadopoulos T.J., *Mycenaean Achaea*, vols. I-II, (SIMA LV:1-2) Göteborg 1978-1979.

Papadopoulos 1989: Papadopoulos T., "Ανασκαφή Καλλιθέας και Κλάους Πατρών", *Prakt* 1989, 57-62 and pls.49-53.

Papadopoulos 1990: Papadopoulos T., "Ανασκαφή Καλλιθέας και Κλάους Πατρών", *Prakt* 1990, 50-55 and pls.27-30.

Papadopoulos 1992: Papadopoulos T., "Ανασκαφή Κλάους και Καλλιθέας Πατρών", *Prakt* 1992, 53-59 and pls.17-19.

Papadopoulou 1997: Papadopoulou E., "Une Tombe à Tholos «Intra Muros». Les Cas du Cimetière MR d' Armenoi", in Driessen J., Farnoux A. (eds.), *La Crète Mycénienne, Actes de la Tâble Rônde Internationale, Organisée par l' École Française d' Athènes, 26-28 Mars 1991* (BCH suppl.30), Athènes 1997, 319-340.

Pariente 1991: Pariente A., "Chronique des Fouilles et Découvertes Archaéologiques en Grèce en 1990", *BCH* 115 (1991), 835-957.

Parlama 1984: Parlama L., *Η Σκύρος στην Εποχή του Χαλκού*, (unpublished D. Phil, Athens University), Athens 1984.

Paschalidis 2001: Paschalidis C.P., "New Pictorial Ceramic Finds from Brauron, Attica: Stylistic Evidence for Local Production", *SMEA* 43 (2001), 93-110.

Paschalidis 2005: Paschalidis C., "Ένας Άγνωστος Μυκηναϊκός «Θησαυρός» από τους Ανδρονιάνους Ευβοίας στο Εθνικό Αρχαιολογικό Μουσείο. Νέα στοιχεία για τη Μεταλλοτεχνία της Μυκηναϊκής Εύβοιας," *to Mouseion* 5 (2005), 29-44.

Paschalidis 2006: Paschalidis C.P., "Elements of Mycenaean Character in Eastern Crete at the End of the Late Bronze Age: Three New Megara in Halasmenos Ierapetra", in Detorakis T., Kalokairinos A. (eds.), *Proceedings of the 9th International Cretological Congress, Elounda, 1-6 October 2001, vol.A1 Prehistoric Period*, Herakleion 2006, 219-232.

Paschalidis 2007: Paschalidis C., "Euboea in the Crossroads of Metals Trade. The Aegean and the Pontic Sea in the Late Bronze Age", in Galanaki I., Tomas H., Galanakis Y, Laffineur R. (eds.), *Between the Aegean and Baltic Seas, Prehistory across the Borders, University of Zagreb, 11-14 April 2005, Zagreb, Mimara Museum, (Aegaeum 27)*, Liège 2007, 433-445, pls. 107-108.

Paschalidis and McGeorge (forthcoming): Paschalidis C., McGeorge P.J.P., "Life and Death in the Periphery of the Mycenaean World at the End of the Late Bronze Age: The Case of the Achaea Klauss Cemetery", in Borgna E. (ed.), *From the Aegean to the Adriatic, Social*

Organizations modes of Exchange and Interaction in the Post-palatial Times (12th-11th BC), International Workshop, Udine, 1-2 December 2006.

Pendlebury 1963: Pendlebury J.D.S., *The Archaeology of Crete. An Introduction*, New York² 1963.

Persson 1931: Persson A.W., *The Royal Tombs at Dendra near Midea*, Lund 1931.

Petroulakis 1915: Petroulakis E.N., "Κρητικής Ατσιπάδας Τάφοι", *ArchEph* 1915, 48-50.

Pini 1968: Pini I., *Beiträge zur Minoischen Gräberkunde*, Wiesbaden 1968.

Piteros 2001: Piteros C.I., "Ταφές και Τεφροδόχα Αγγεία Τύμβου της ΥΕ ΙΙΙΓ στο Άργος", in Stampolidis N.C. (ed.), *Proceedings of the Symposium: Crematios in the Bronze and the Early Iron Age. Rhodes, 29 April – 2 May1999*, Athens 2001, 99-120.

Platon 1953: Platon N., "Η Αρχαιολογική Κίνησις εν Κρήτη κατά το Έτος 1953", *CretChron* 7 (1953), 439-492.

Platon 1959: Platon N., "Ανασκαφή Αχλαδιών Σητείας", *Prakt* 1959, 210-219.

Platon 1959a: Platon N., "Η Αρχαιολογική Κίνησις εν Κρήτη κατά το Έτος 1959", *CretChron* 13 (1959), 359-393.

Platon 1960: Platon N., "Ανασκαφή Περιοχής Πραισού", *Prakt* 1960, 294-307.

Platon and Davaras 1960: Platon N., Davaras C., "Η Αρχαιολογική Κίνησις εν Κρήτη κατά το Έτος 1960", *CretChron* 14 (1960), 504-527.

Popham 1965: Popham M.R., "Some Late Minoan III Pottery from Crete", *BSA* 60 (1965), 316-342, pls. 81-86.

Popham 1967: Popham M., "Late Minoan Pottery. A Summary", *BSA* 62 (1967), 337-351, pls. 76-90.

Popham 1970: Popham M.R., *The Destruction of the Palace at Knossos. Pottery of the Late Minoan IIIA Period*, (SIMA XII) Göteborg 1970.

Popham 1984: Popham M.R., *The Minoan Unexplored Mansion at Knossos*, vols. I-II, (BSA suppl.17) Oxford 1984.

Popham 1994: Popham M.R., "Late Minoan II to the End of the Bronze Age", in Evely D., Hughes-Brock H., Momigliano N. (eds.), *Knossos. A Labyrinth of History. Papers Presented in Honour of Singlair Hood*, Oxford 1994, 89-102, pls. 6-12.

Preston Day 1997: Preston Day L., "The Late Minoan IIIC Period at Vronda, Kavousi", in Driessen J., Farnoux A. (eds.), *La Crète Mycénienne, Actes de la Tâble Rônde Internationale, Organisée par l' École Française d' Athènes, 26-28 Mars 1991* (BCH suppl.30), Athènes 1997, 391-406.

Protopapadaki 1999: Protopapadaki E., "Small Jug", in Tzedakis Y., Martlew H. (eds.), *Minoans and Mycenaeans, Flavours of Their Times* (Exhibition Catalogue), Athens 1999, 241.

Rethemiotakis 1997: Rethemiotakis G., 'Late Minona III Pottery from Kastelli Pediada', in Hallager E., Hallager B.P. (eds.), *Late Minoan Pottery Chronology and Terminology, Acts of a Meeting held at the Danish Institute at Athens, August 12-14, 1994*, Athens 1997, 305-336.

Rethemiotakis 1997a: Rethemiotakis G., 'A Chest-Shaped Vessel from Kastelli Pediada' in Driessen J., Farnoux A. (eds.), *La Crète Mycénienne, Actes de la Tâble Rônde Internationale, Organisée par l' École Française d' Athènes, 26-28 Mars 1991* (BCH suppl.30), Athènes 1997, 407-421.

Robinson 1942: Robinson D.M., *Excavations at Olynthus XI*, Baltimore 1942.

Rutter and Van de Moortel: Rutter J.B., Van de Moortel A., "Minoan Pottery from the Southern Area", in Shaw J.W., Shaw M.C. (eds.) *Kommos V. The Monumental Minoan Buildings at Kommos*, Princeton 2006, 261-715.

Sakellarakis 1992: Sakellarakis J.A., *The Mycenaean Pictorial Style in the National Archaeological Museum of Athens*, Athens 1992.

Sakellarakis and Sakellaraki 1997: Sakellarakis Y.A., Sapouna-Sakellaraki E., *Αρχάνες. Minoan Crete in a New Light*, vols. I-II, Athens 1997.

Seager 1909: Seager R.B., "Excavations on the Island of Mochlos, Crete, in 1908", *AJA* 13 (1909), 273-303.

Seager 1912: Seager R.B., *Explorations in the Island of Mochlos*, Boston and New York 1912.

Seiradaki 1960: Seiradaki M., "Pottery from Karphi", *BSA* 55 (1960), 1-37, pls.1-14.

Shelton 1996: Shelton K.S., *The Late Helladic Pottery from Prosymna*, (SIMA pocket-book 138), Jonsered 1996.

Shipman, Foster and Schoeninger 1984: Shipman P., Foster G. and Schoeninger M., "Burnt Bones and Teeth: an Experimental Study of Colour, Morphology, Crystal Structure and shrinkage", *JAS* 2 (1984), 307-325.

Smith 2002: Smith R.A.K., *The Tombs of Mochlos and Myrsini: Pottery and Cultural Regionalism in Late Minoan III Crete*, (unpublished D. Phil, Bryn Mawr College, December 2002).

Smith 2004: Smith R.A.K., "Late Minoan III Mochlos and the Regional Consumption of Pottery", in Preston Day L., Mook M.S., Muhly J.D. (eds), *Crete Beyond the Palaces: Proccedings of the Crete 2000 Conference*, Philadelphia 2004, 309-317.

Smith 2005: Smith R.A., "Minoans, Mycenaeans and Mochlos: The Formation of Regional Identity in Late Minoan III Crete", in D'Agata A.L., Moody J., Williams E. (eds.), *Ariadne's Threads. Connections between Crete and the Greek Mainland in Late Minoan III (LM IIIA2 to LM IIIC), Proceedings of the International Workshop held at Athens, Scuola Archeologica Italiana, 5-6 April 2003*, Atene 2005, 185-204.

Soles and Davaras 1996: Soles J., Davaras C., "Excavations at Mochlos, 1992-1993", *Hesperia* 65 (1996), 175-230.

Soles and Davaras 2008: Soles J.S. and Davaras C. (eds.), *Mochlos IIA, Period IV. The Mycenaean Settlement and Cemetery. The Sites*, Philadelphia 2008.

Souyoudzoglou-Haywood 1999: Souyoudzoglou-Haywood C., *The Ionian Islands in the Bronze Age and Early Iron Age 3000-800 BC*, Liverpool 1999.

Spyropoulos 1972: Spyropoulos T.G., Υστερομυκηναϊκοί Ελλαδικοί Θησαυροί, Athens 1972.

Themelis 1980: Themelis P.G., "The Burial Customs", in Popham M.R., Sackett L.H., Themelis P.G. (eds.), *Lefkandi I, the Iron Age*, (BSA suppl.11) London 1980, 209-216.

Thomas 1997: Thomas P.M., "Mycenaean Kylix Painters at Zygouries", in Laffineur R., Betancourt P.P. (eds.), *TEXNH, Craftsmen, Craftswomen and Craftsmanship in the Aegean Bronze Age, Proceedings of the 6th International Aegean Conference, Philadelphia, Temple University, 18-21 April 1996 (Aegaeum 16)*, I-II, Liège 1997, 377-383, pls.156-158.

Thomatos 2006: Thomatos M., *The Final Revival of the Aegean Bronze Age. A Case Study of the Argolid, Corinthia, Attica, Euboea, the Cyclades and the Dodecanese during LH IIIC Middle*, (BAR Int.Series 1498), Oxford 2006.

Triantafyllidis 2002-2005: Triantafyllidis P., "Γυάλινα και Φαγεντιανά Κοσμήματα Αρμενοχωρίου Αστυπάλαιας", *AAA* 35-38 (2002-2005), 165-184.

Tsipopoulou 1992: Tsipopoulou M., "Jug", in Marangou L. (ed.), *Minoan and Greek Civilization from the Mitsotakis Collection*, Athens 1992, 278.

Tsipopoulou 1995: Tsipopoulou M., "Late Minoan III Sitia. Patterns of Settlement and Land Use", in Tsipopoulou M., Vagnetti L., *ACHLADIA. Scavi e Ricerche della Missione Greco-Italiana in Creta Orientale (1991-1993)*, Roma 1995, 177-192.

Tsipopoulou 1997: Tsipopoulou M., "Late Minoan III Reoccupation in the Area of the Palatial Building at Petras, Siteia", in Hallager E., Hallager B.P. (eds.), *Late Minoan Pottery Chronology and Terminology, Acts of a Meeting held at the Danish Institute at Athens, August 12-14, 1994*, Athens 1997, 209-257.

Tsipopoulou 2005: Tsipopoulou M., "'Mycenoans' at the Isthmus of Ierapetra: Some (Preliminary) Thoughts on the Foundation of the (Eteo)Cretan Cultural Identity", in D'Agata A.L., Moody J., Williams E. (eds.), *Ariadne's Threads. Connections between Crete and the Greek Mainland in Late Minoan III (LM IIIA2 to LM IIIC), Proceedings of the International Workshop held at Athens, Scuola*

Archeologica Italiana, 5-6 April 2003, Atene 2005, 303-333.

Tsipopoulou and Little 2001: Τσιποπούλου Μ., Little L., "Καύσεις του Τέλους της Εποχής του Χαλκού στην Κριτσά Μιραμπέλλου, Ανατολική Κρήτη", in Stampolidis N.C. (ed.), *Proceedings of the Symposium: Crematios in the Bronze and the Early Iron Age. Rhodes, 29 April – 2 May1999,* Athens 2001, 83-98.

Tsipopoulou and Vagnetti 1997: Tsipopoulou M., Vagnetti L., "Workshop Attributions for some Late Minoan III East Cretan Larnakai", in Laffineur R., Betancourt P.P. (eds.), *TEXNH, Craftsmen, Craftswomen and Craftsmanship in the Aegean Bronze Age, Proceedings of the 6th International Aegean Conference, Philadelphia, Temple University, 18-21 April 1996 (Aegaeum 16),* τ.I-II, Liège 1997, 473-479, pls.180-188.

Tsipopoulou and Vagnetti 1999: Tsipopoulou M., Vagnetti L., "A Bath-Tub Larnax from Tourloti (Sitia), East Crete", *SMEA* 41 (1999), 123-143.

Tsipopoulou and Vagnetti 2006: Tsipopoulou M., Vagnetti L., "Late Minoan III Evidence from Kritsa, Mirabello", in Detorakis T., Kalokairinos A. (eds.), *Proceedings of the 9th International Cretological Congress, Elounda, 1-6 October 2001, vol. A1 Prehistoric Period,* Ηράκλειο 2006, 201-210.

Tzedakis 1969: Tzedakis I., "L' Atelier de Céramique Postpalatiale à Kydônia", *BCH* 93 (1969), 396-418.

Vagnetti 2000-2001: Vagnetti L., "Preliminary Remarks on Mycenaean Pictorial Pottery from the Central Mediterranean", *OpAth* 25-26 (2000-2001), 107-115.

Van Effenterre 1948: Van Effenterre H., *Nécropoles du Mirabello,* (Etudes Crétoises 8), Paris 1948.

Vermeule and Karageorghis 1982: Vermeule E., Karageorghis V., *Mycenaean Pictorial Vase Painting,* Cambridge, Massachusetts and London 1982.

Vlachopoulos 1995: Vlachopoulos A., "Ψευδόστομος Αμφορέας του Πολυποδικού Ρυθμού στο Μουσείο της Πύλου", *ArchEph* 134 (1995), 247-256, pl.66.

Vlachopoulos 1995a: Vlachopoulos A., *Η Υστεροελλαδική III Γ Περίοδος στη Νάξο. Τα Ταφικά Σύνολα και οι Συσχετισμοί τους με το Αιγαίο,* (unpublished D. Phil, Athens University, vols I-II, 1995).

Vlachopoulos 2006: Vlachopoulos A.G., *Η Υστεροελλαδική IIIΓ Περίοδος στη Νάξο. Τα Ταφικά Σύνολα και οι Συσχετισμοί τους με το Αιγαίο,* vol. A, Athens 2006.

Vlachopoulos 2006a: Vlachopoulos A., "Δίδυμοι Ψευδόστομοι Αμφορείς του Αργολικού Πολυποδικού-Πυκνού Ρυθμού", in Kazakou M. (ed.), *Proceedings of the 1st Archaeological Conference of South and Western Greece, Patras 9-12 June 1996,* Athens 2006, 179-192.

Warren 1997: Warren P.M., "Late Minoan III Pottery from the City of Knossos: Stratigraphical museum Extension Site" in Hallager E., Hallager B.P. (eds.), *Late Minoan Pottery Chronology and Terminology, Acts of a Meeting held at the Danish Institute at Athens, August 12-14, 1994,* Athens 1997, 157-192.

Watrous 1992: Watrous L.V., *Kommos III. The Late Bronze Age Pottery,* Princeton 1992.

Weiner 1951: Weiner J.S., "Cremated Remains from Dorchester", in Atkinson R.J.C., Piggot C.M. and Sandars N.K., *Excavations at Dorchester,* Oxford 1951, 129-141.

Wells 1960: Wells C., "A Study of Cremation", *Antiquity* 34 (1960), 29-37.

Xanthoudidis 1904: Xanthoudidis S.A., "Εκ Κρήτης", *ArchEph* 1904, 1-56, πιν.1-3.

Xanthoudidis 1904a: Xanthoudidis S.A., *Κρητικός Πολιτισμός, Ήτοι τα Εξαγόμενα των εν Κρήτη Ανασκαφών,* Athens 1904.

Xanthoudidis 1906: Xanthoudidis S.A., 'Εκ Κρήτης', *ArchEph* 1906, 117-156, πιν.7-11.

Xenaki 1950: Xenaki A., "Όπλα και Εργαλεία της Συλλογής Γιαμαλάκη", *CretChron* 4 (1950), 107-128.

Xenaki-Sakellariou 1985: Xenaki-Sakellariou A., *Οι Θαλαμωτοί Τάφοι των Μυκηνών Ανασκαφής Χρ. Τσούντα (1887-1898),* Paris 1985.

Zois 1996: Zois A.A., *Κνωσός. Το Εκστατικό Όραμα. Σημειωτική και Ψυχολογία μιας Αρχαιολογικής Περιπέτειας*, Herakleion 1996.

List of plates and figures

Plate 1a. View from the East of the village of Tourloti and of the hillside dropping down to Mochlos (photograph by Kleio Zervaki).

Plate 1b. The vases and small finds from the chamber tomb excavated by Nikos Papadakis.

Plate 2a. The vases presented by Manolis Fygetakis.

Plate 2b. The two vases from the chamber tomb excavated by Metaxia Tsipopoulou.

Plate 3a. Stirrup-jar CAM 484 (Photograph by Giorgos Fafalis; courtesy of the Museum of Cycladic Art – N.P. Goulandris Foundation).

Plate 3b. Stirrup-jar CAM 484 (Photograph by Giorgos Fafalis; courtesy of the Museum of Cycladic Art – N.P. Goulandris Foundation).

Plate 4a-b. Stirrup-jar **SM 4026**.

Plate 4c. Spindle whorls and bead from the chamber tomb excavated by N. Papadakis.

Plate 4d. Stirrup-jars T87/3 and T15/2 from Ialysos, Rhodes (courtesy of the 22nd Ephorate of Prehistoric and Classical Antiquities, Rhodes).

Figure 1. Jewellery and small finds from the chamber tomb excavated by M. Mavroeidis in 1936 (after Mavroeidis 1938, 218).

Figure 2. Plan of the chamber tomb excavated by M. Tsipopoulou.

Figure 3. Three-handled piriform jar or small krater **SM 4511**.

Figure 4. Three-handled piriform jar or small krater **SM 4511**.

Figure 5. Trefoil spouted jug **SM 4512**.

Figure 6. Trefoil spouted jug **SM 4512**.

Figure 7. Calcified remains of a fine textile on the belly of the trefoil jug **SM 4512**.

Figure 8. Stirrup-jar **SM 5071**.

Figure 9. Stirrup-jar **SM 5071**.

Figure 10. Stirrup-jar **SM 5071**.

Figure 11. The octopus composition on stirrup-jar **SM 5071**.

Figure 12. Stirrup-jar **SM 5072**.

Figure 13. Stirrup-jar **SM 5072**.

Figure 14. Stirrup-jar **SM 5072**.

Figure 15. Stirrup-jar **SM 5073**.

Figure 16. Stirrup-jar **SM 5073**.

Figure 17. Stirrup-jar **SM 5073**.

Figure 18. Stirrup-jar **SM 5074**.

Figure 19. Stirrup-jar **SM 5074**.

Figure 20. Stirrup-jar **SM 5074**. The shoulder's main decorative motif.

Figure 21. Stirrup-jar **SM 5074**.

Figure 22. Lid **SM 5075**.

Figure 23. Lid **SM 5075**.

Figure 24. Lid **SM 5075**.

Figure 25. Lid **SM 5075**.

Figure 26. Stamnos **SM 5078**, with the burnt bones of a man and a child.

Figure 27. Stamnos **SM 5078**.

Figure 28. Spindle whorls **SM 5079** and **SM 5080**.

Figure 29. Faience bead **SM 5081**.

Figure 30. Jug **SM 4023**.

Figure 31. Jug **SM 4023**.

Figure 32. Beak-spouted juglet **SM 4024**.

Figure 33. Beak-spouted juglet **SM 4024**.

Figure 34. Stirrup-jar **SM 4025**.

Figure 35. Stirrup-jar **SM 4025**.

Figure 36. Stirrup-jar **SM 4025**.

Figure 37. Stirrup-jar **SM 4027**.

Figure 38. Stirrup-jar **SM 4027**.

Figure 39. Stirrup-jar **SM 4027**.

Figure 40. Stirrup-jar **SM 4028**.

Figure 41. Stirrup-jar **SM 4028**.

Figure 42. Stirrup-jar **SM 4028**.

Figure 43. Trefoil spouted jugs **NAM 14624, 14625 and 14626** (Photograph by Irini Kapiri; courtesy of the Photographic Archive of the National Archaeological Museum).

Figure 44. Trefoil spouted jugs **NAM 14624, 14625 and 14626** (Photograph by Irini Kapiri; courtesy of the Photographic Archive of the National Archaeological Museum).

Figure 45. Trefoil spouted jug **NAM 14624**.

Figure 46. Trefoil spouted jug **NAM 14625**.

Figure 47. Trefoil spouted jug **NAM 14626**.

Figure 48. Stirrup-jar **SM 4026**.

Figure 49. Stirrup-jar **SM 4026**.

Figure 50. Stirrup-jar **SM 4026**.

Figure 51. Stirrup-jar **SM 4026**. The eye-like ornament on the backside of the octopus composition.

Figure 52. Stirrup-jar **SM 4026**.

Figure 53. Stirrup-jar **SM 4026**. The octopus composition on the shoulder.

Figure 54. Stirrup-jar **HM 3480** from Tholos Tomb B at Mouliana (courtesy of Dr Colin Macdonald).

Figure 55. Stirrup-jar **HM 3480**. Detail of the octopus decoration (courtesy of Dr Colin Macdonald).

Figure 56. Stirrup-jar **HM 3480** (after Kanta 1980, fig.82:5-6).

Figure 57. Stirrup-jar **HM 3480**. The octopus decoration on the shoulder (after Xanthoudidis 1904, pl.1; courtesy of the Athens Archaeological Society).

Figure 58. Stirrup-jar **HM 3481** from Tholos Tomb B at Mouliana (courtesy of Dr Colin Macdonald).

Figure 59. Stirrup-jar **HM 3481**. Detail of the octopus decoration (courtesy of Dr Colin Macdonald).

Figure 60. Stirrup-jar **HM 3481** (after Kanta 1980, fig.82:8-9).

Figure 61. Stirrup-jar **HM 3481**. The decoration on the shoulder (after Xanthoudidis 1904, pl.1; courtesy of the Athens Archaeological Society).

Figure 62. Stirrup-jar **CAM 484**.

Figure 63. Stirrup-jar **CAM 484**. The decoration on the shoulder.

Figure 64. Stirrup-jar **NM 914** from Aplomata, Naxos (after Vlachopoulos 2006, pl.106; courtesy of the author).

Figure 65. Stirrup-jar **NM 914** from Aplomata, Naxos (after Vlachopoulos 2006, pl.106; courtesy of the author).

Figure 66. Stirrup-jar **NM 914**. The octopus decoration on the shoulder (after Vlachopoulos 2006, 338 fig.93; courtesy of the author).

Figure 67. Larnax 23436 of the Musée d' Art et d' Histoire, Ville de Genève (Photograph by Yves Siza; courtesy of the Photographic Service of the Museum).

Figure 68. Fragments of stirrup-jars of the Close Octopus and Fringed Style from Kavousi-Vronda (after Preston Day 1997, 397 fig.4; courtesy of the author).

Figure 69. Stirrup-jar **ANM 180** from Kritsa. The octopus decoration on the shoulder (after Kanta 1980, fig.136:1).

Figure 70. Stirrup-jar from Vassiliki, Ierapetra (after Popham 1967, pl.89:f; courtesy of the Archive of the British School at Athens).

Figure 71. Fragments of a stirrup-jar from Thronos/Kefala, Amari (after D'Agata 1999, 191 fig.6:3.20; courtesy of the author).

Figure 72. Cremation in the urn.

Figure 73. Frontal bone fragments.

Figure 74. Occipital bone fragments.

Figure 75. Basi-occipital, petrous and sphenoid bones.

Figure 76. Right temporal and mandible fragments.

Figure 77. Tooth roots.

Figure 78. Right clavicle.

Figure 79. Left clavicle.

Figure 80. Left scapula fragments.

Figure 81. Left and right humerus fragments.

Figure 82. Left humerus.

Figure 83. Radiuses.

Figure 84. Carpals.

Figure 85. Metacarpals.

Figure 86. Metacarpal, seriously warped.

Figure 87. Phalanges.

Figure 88. Thumb.

Figure 89. Pelvis and sacrum fragment.

Figure 90. Fibula shaft and femur condyle.

Figure 91. Distal fibula.

Figure 92. Axis and a cervical body.

Figure 93. Thoracic fragments.

Figure 94. Lumbars.

Figure 95. Lumbar.

Figure 96. Ribs.

Figure 97. Child's molar.

Figure 98. Child's lumbar.

Figure 99. Adult and child lumbars juxtaposed.

Figure 100. Sheep/goat premolar tooth fragment.

Plate 1

Plate 1a. View from the East of the village of Tourloti and of the hillside dropping down to Mochlos.

Plate 1b. The vases and small finds from the chamber tomb excavated by Nikos Papadakis.

Plate 2

Plate 2a. The vases presented by Manolis Fygetakis.

Plate 2b. The two vases from the chamber tomb excavated by Metaxia Tsipopoulou.

Plate 3

Plate 3a. Stirrup-jar CAM 484.

Plate 3b. Stirrup-jar CAM 484.

Plate 4

Plate 4a-b. Stirrup-jar **SM 4026**.

Plate 4c. Spindle whorls and bead from the chamber tomb excavated by N. Papadakis

Plate 4d. Stirrup-jars T87/3 and T15/2 from Ialysos, Rhodes.

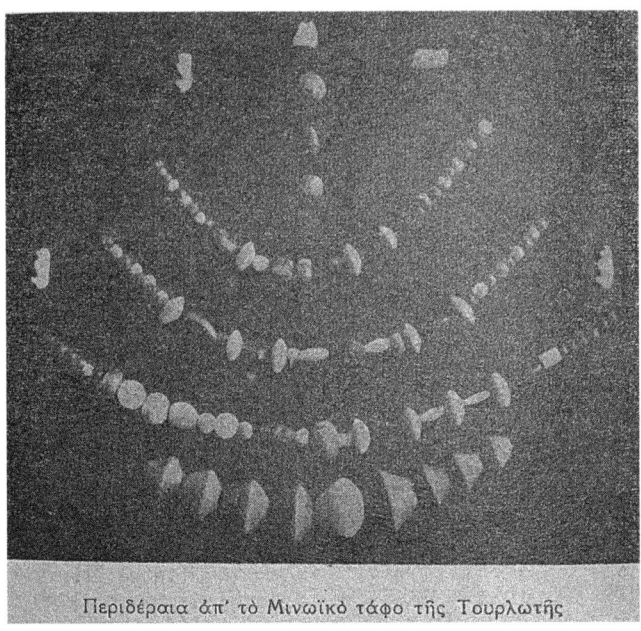

Figure 1. Jewellery and small finds from the chamber tomb excavated by M. Mavroeidis in 1936.

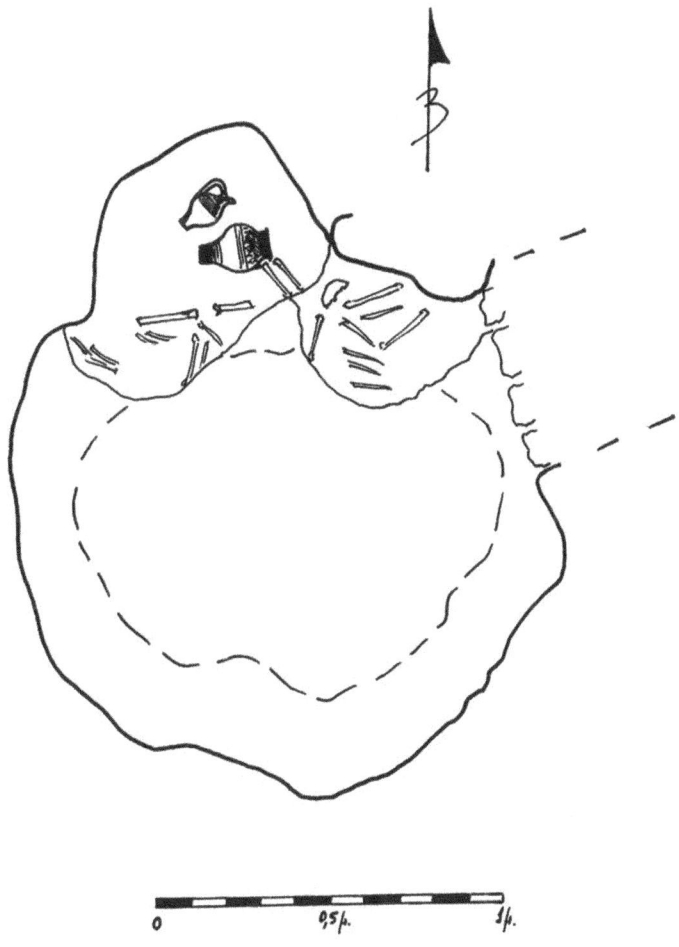

Figure 2. Plan of the chamber tomb excavated by M. Tsipopoulou.

Figure 3. Three-handled piriform jar or small krater **SM 4511.**

Figure 4. Three-handled piriform jar or small krater **SM 4511.**

Figure 5. Trefoil spouted jug **SM 4512**.

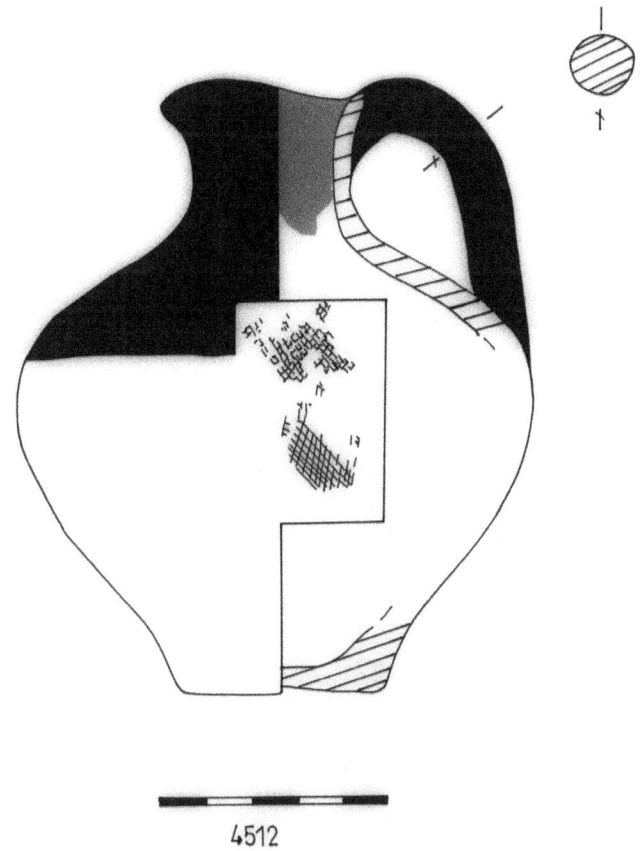

Figure 6. Trefoil spouted jug **SM 4512**.

Figure 7. Calcified remains of a fine textile on the belly of the trefoil jug **SM 4512.**

Figure 8. Stirrup-jar **SM 5071.**

Figure 9. Stirrup-jar **SM 5071.**

Figure 10. Stirrup-jar **SM 5071.**

Figure 11. The octopus decoration on stirrup-jar **SM 5071.**

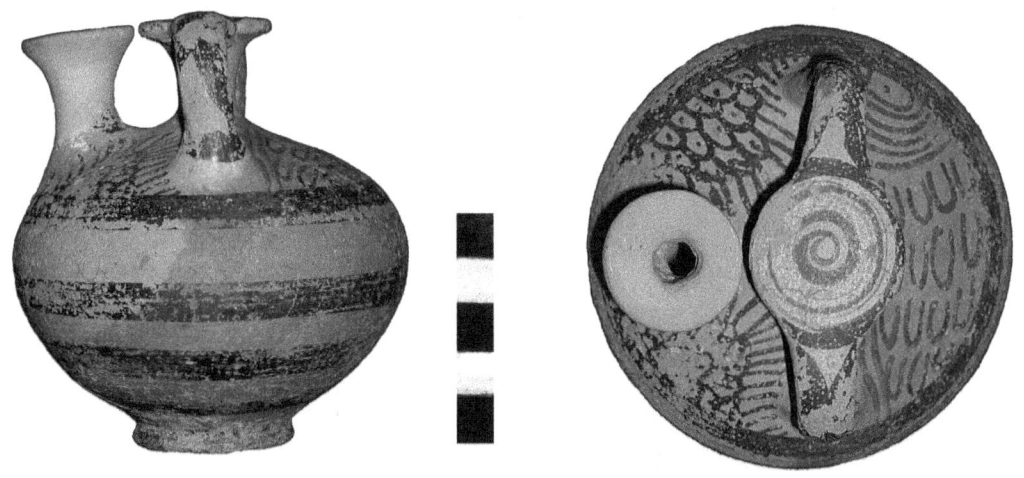

Figures 12 and 13. Stirrup-jar SM 5072.

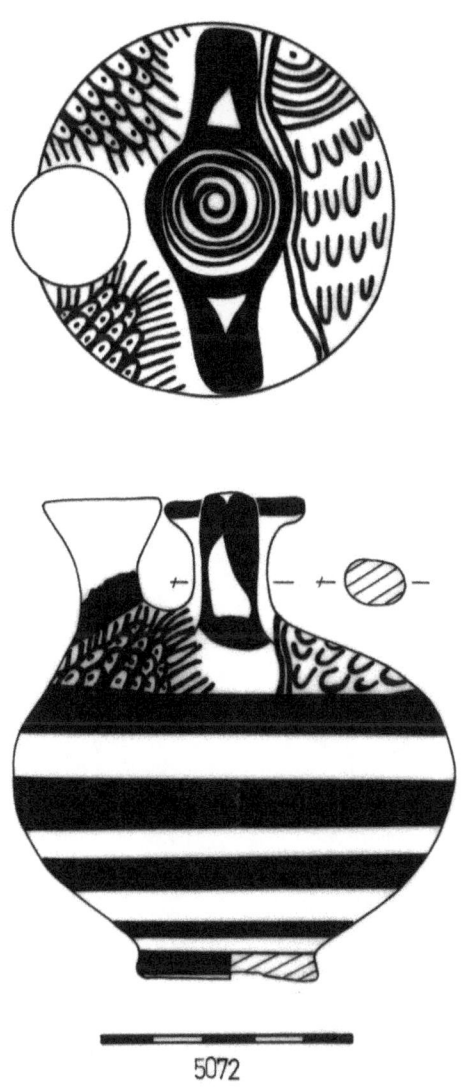

Figure 14. Stirrup-jar SM 5072.

Figure 15. Stirrup-jar **SM 5073.**

Figure 16. Stirrup-jar **SM 5073.**

Figure 17. Stirrup-jar **SM 5073.**

Figure 18. Stirrup-jar SM 5074.

Figure 19. Stirrup-jar SM 5074.

Figure 20. Stirrup-jar **SM 5074.** The shoulder's main decorative motif.

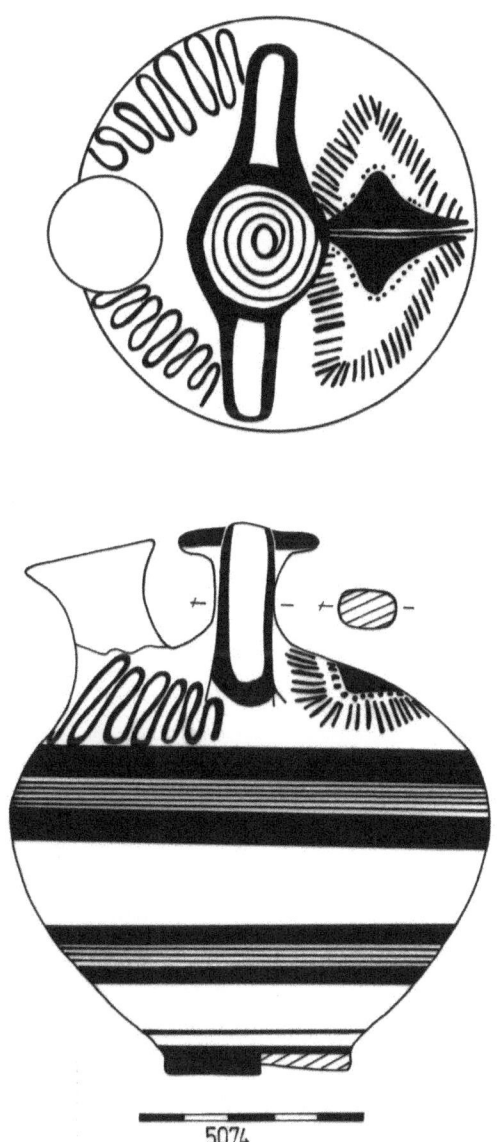

Figure 21. Stirrup-jar **SM 5074.**

Figure 22. Lid SM 5075.

Figure 23. Lid SM 5075.

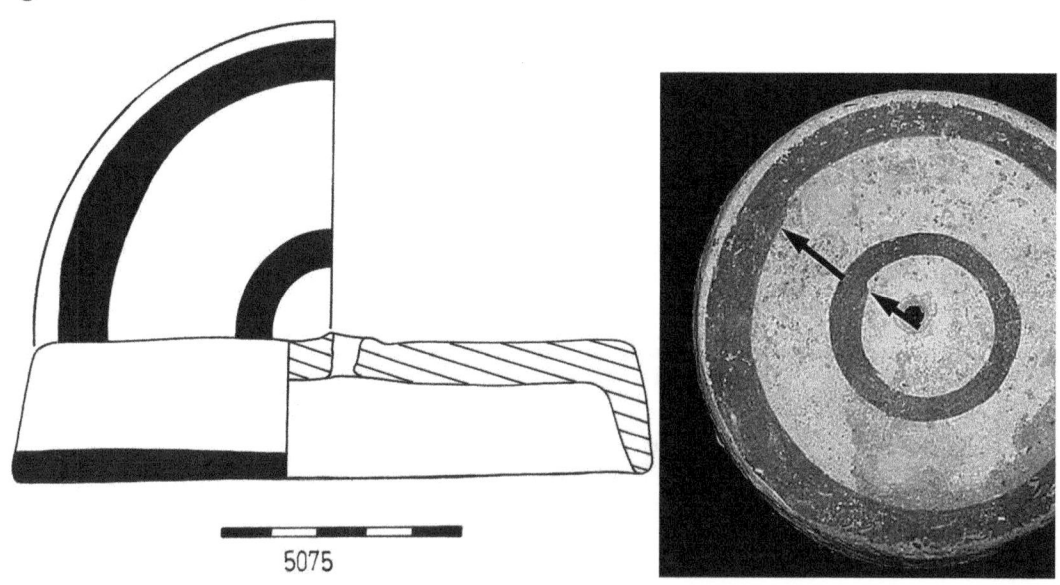

Figures 24, 25. Lid SM 5075.

Figure 26. Stamnos **SM 5078**, with the burnt bones of a man and a child.

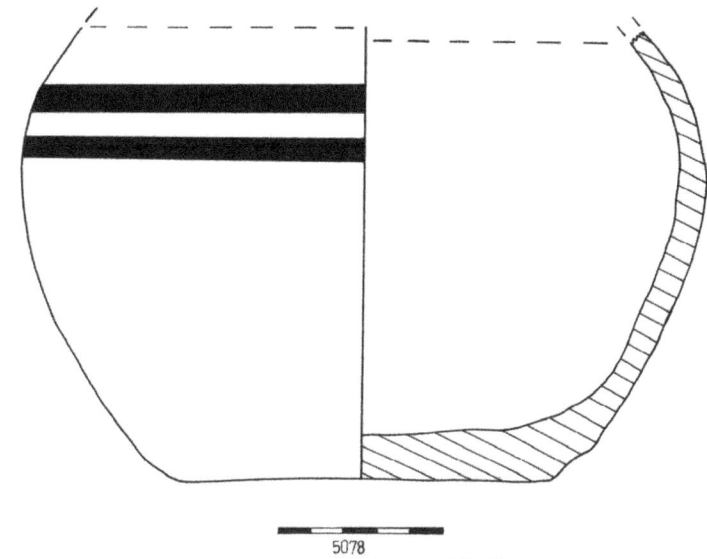

Figure 27. Stamnos **SM 5078**.

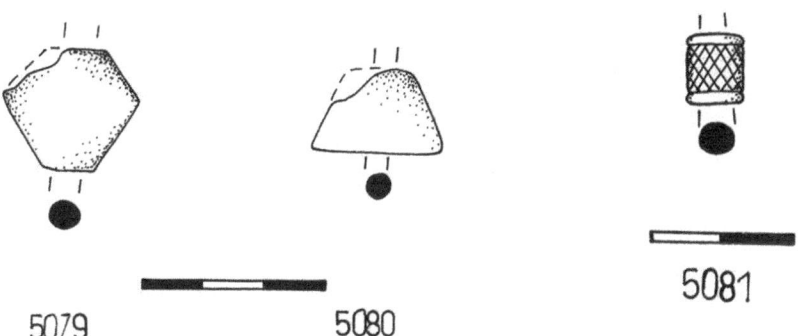

Figure 28. Spindle whorls **SM 5079** and **SM 5080**.

Figure 29. Faience bead **SM 5081**.

Figure 30. Jug SM 4023.

Figure 31. Jug SM 4023.

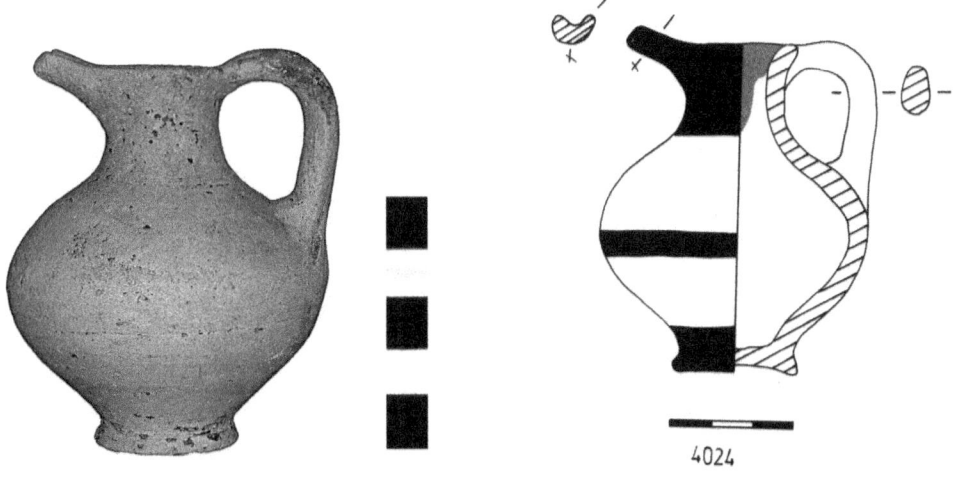

Figures 32 and 33. Beak-spouted juglet **SM 4024.**

Figure 34. Stirrup-jar **SM 4025.**

Figure 35. Stirrup-jar SM **4025.**

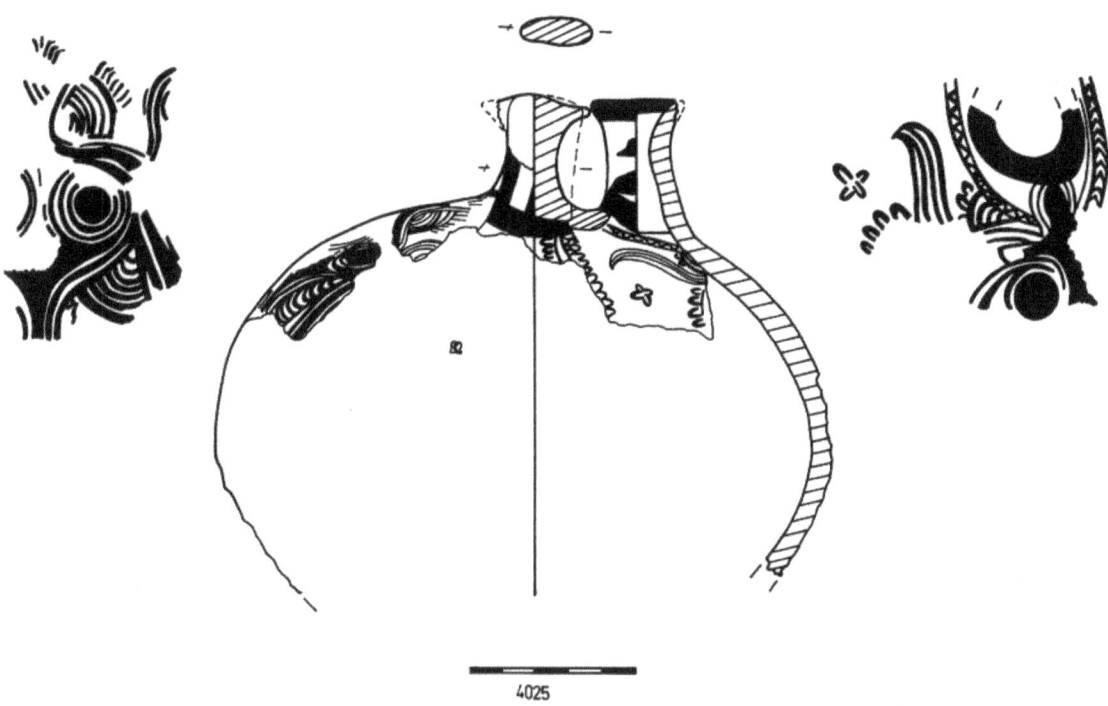

Figure 36. Stirrup-jar SM **4025.**

Figures 37 and 38. Stirrup-jar SM **4027.**

Figure 39. Stirrup-jar SM **4027.**

Figures 40 and 41. Stirrup-jar SM 4028.

Figure 42. Stirrup-jar SM 4028.

Figure 43. Trefoil spouted jugs **NAM 14624, 14625 and 14626.**

Figure 44. Trefoil spouted jugs **NAM 14624, 14625 and 14626.**

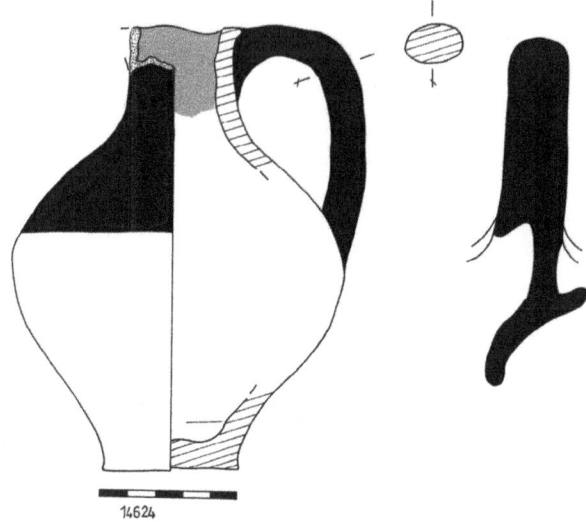

Figure 45. Trefoil spouted jug **NAM 14624**.

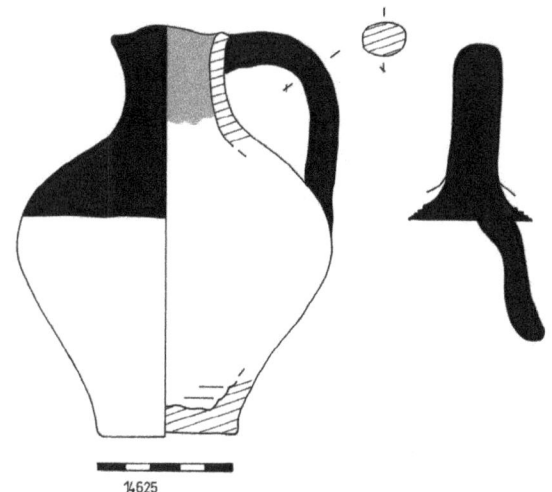

Figure 46. Trefoil spouted jug **NAM 14625**.

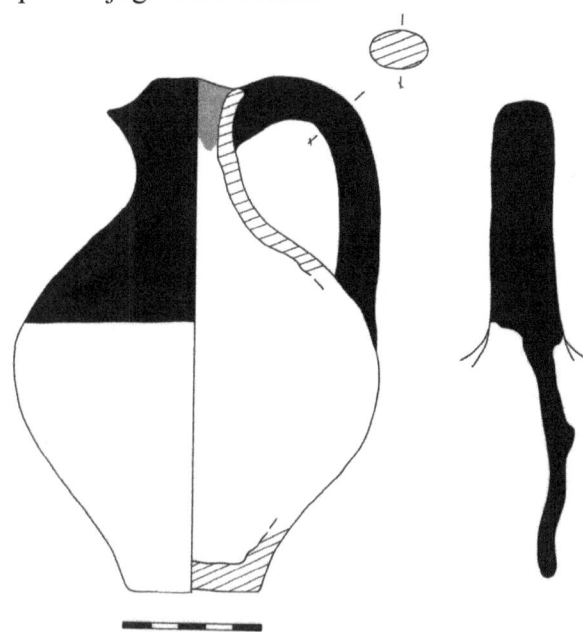

Figure 47. Trefoil spouted jug **NAM 14626**.

Figure 48. Stirrup-jar SM 4026.

Figure 49. Stirrup-jar SM 4026.

Figure 50. Stirrup-jar **SM 4026.**

Figure 51. Stirrup-jar **SM 4026.** The eye-like ornament on the backside of the octopus composition.

Figure 52. Stirrup-jar **SM 4026.**

Figure 53. Stirrup-jar **SM 4026.** The octopus decoration on the shoulder.

Figure 54. Stirrup-jar **HM 3480** from Tholos Tomb B at Mouliana.

Figure 55. Stirrup-jar **HM 3480.** Detail of the octopus decoration.

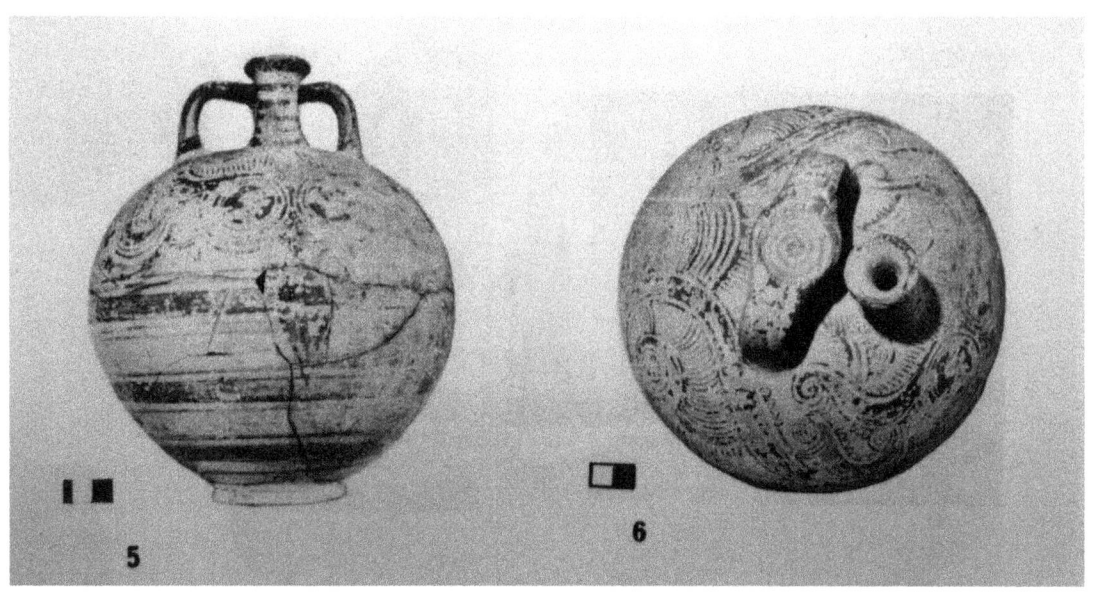

Figure 56. Stirrup-jar **HM 3480.**

Figure 57. Stirrup-jar **HM 3480.** The octopus decoration on the shoulder.

Figure 58. Stirrup-jar **HM 3481** from Tholos Tomb B at Mouliana.

Figure 59. Stirrup-jar **HM 3481.** Detail of the octopus decoration.

Figure 60. Stirrup-jar **HM 3481.**

Figure 61. Stirrup-jar **HM 3481.** The decoration on the shoulder.

Figure 62. Stirrup-jar **CAM 484.**

Figure 63. Stirrup-jar **CAM 484.** The decoration on the shoulder.

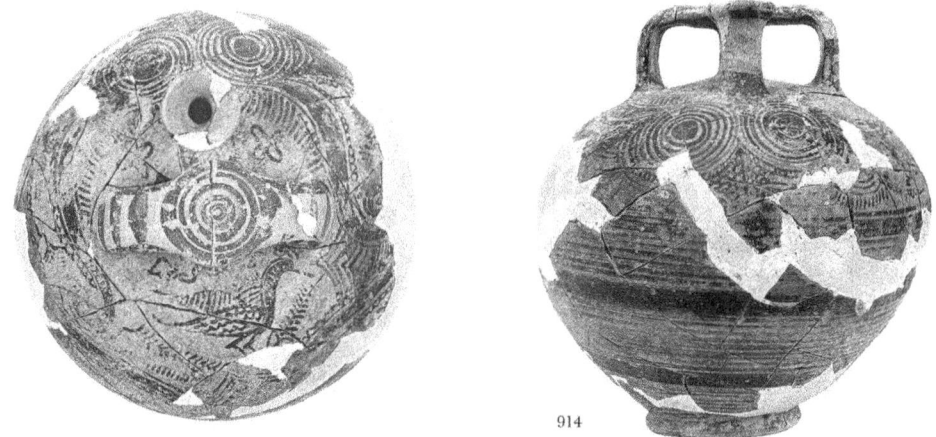

Figures 64 and 65. Stirrup-jar **NM 914** from Aplomata, Naxos.

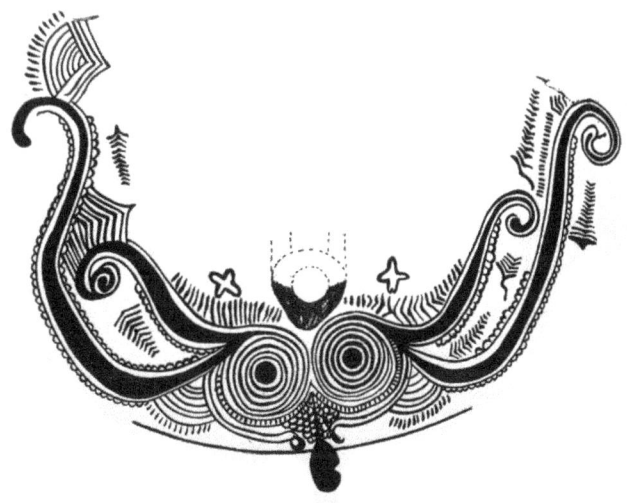

Figure 66. Stirrup-jar **NM 914.** The octopus decoration on the shoulder.

Figure 67. Larnax 23436 of the Musée d' Art et d' Histoire, Ville de Genève.

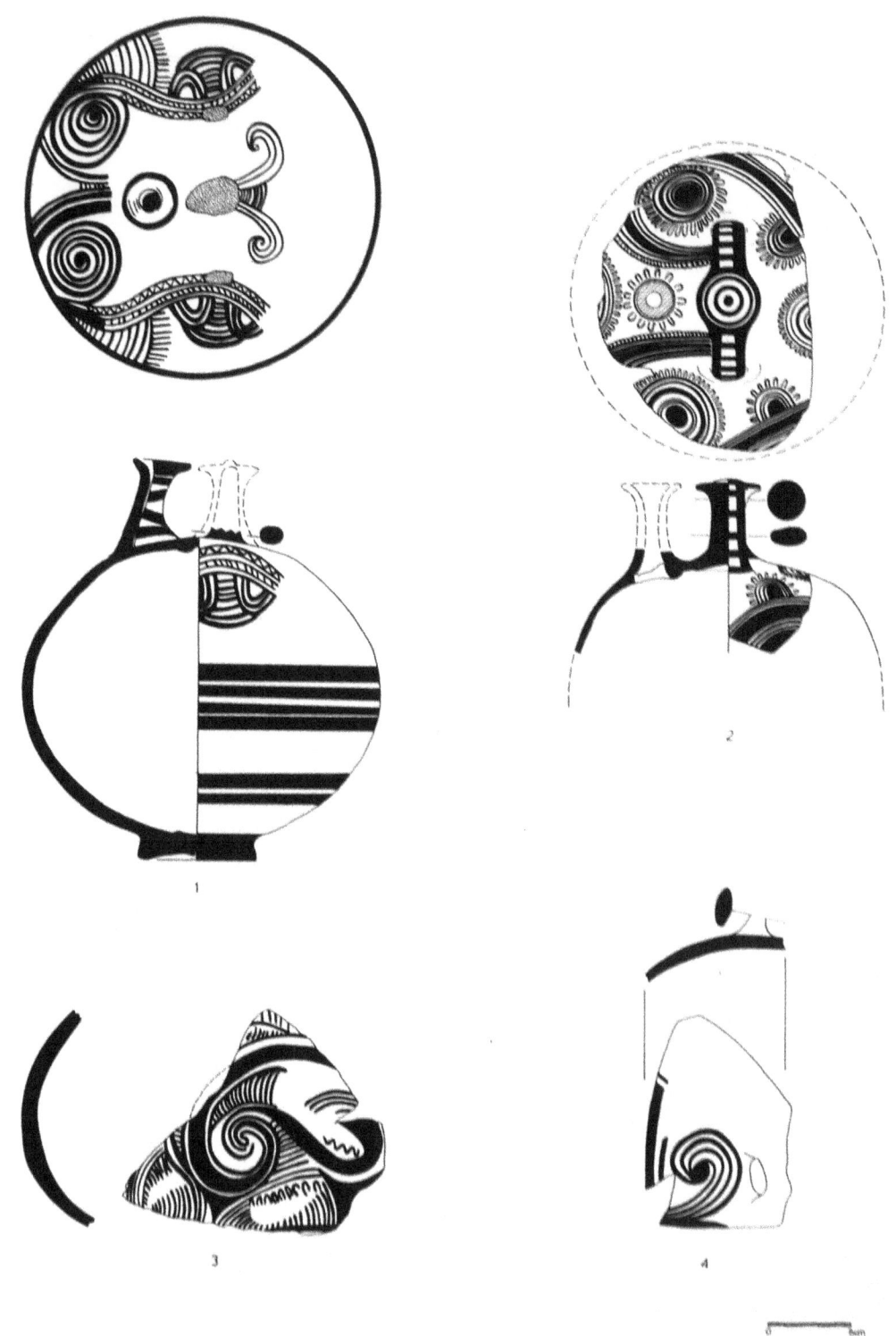

Figure 68. Fragments of stirrup-jars of the Close Octopus and Fringed Style from Kavousi-Vronda.

Figure 69. Stirrup-jar **ANM 180** from Kritsa. The octopus decoration on the shoulder.

Figure 70. Stirrup-jar from Vassiliki, Ierapetra.

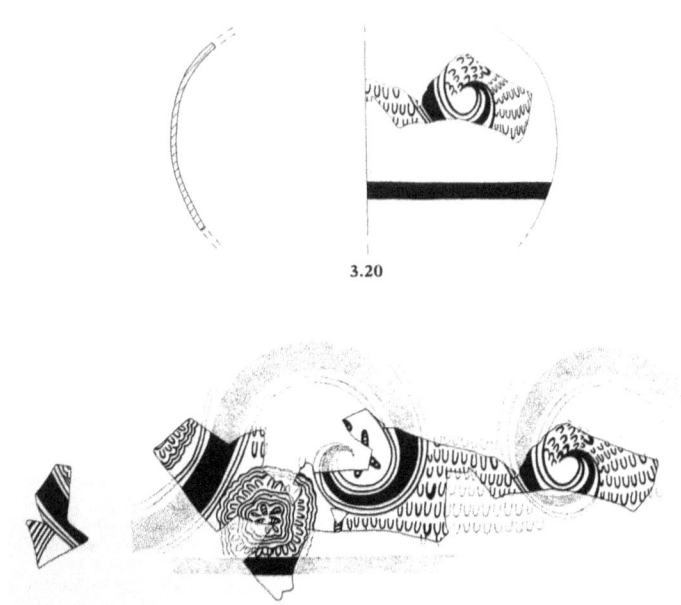

Figure 71. Fragments of a stirrup-jar from Thronos/Kefala, Amari.

Figure 72. Cremation in the urn.

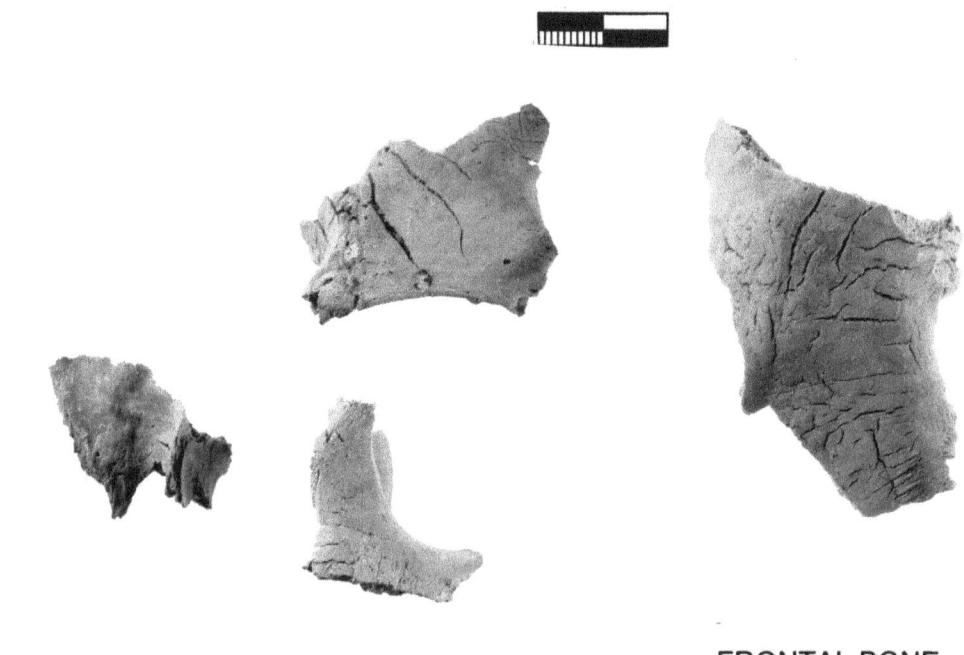

FRONTAL BONE

Figure 73. Frontal bone fragments.

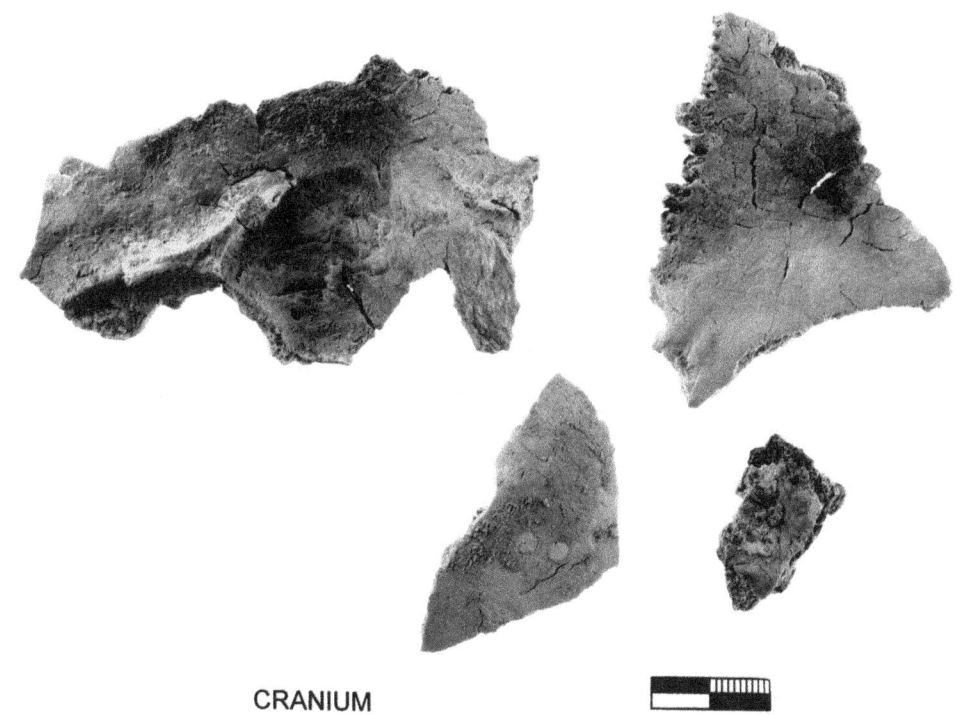

Figure 74. Occipital bone fragments.

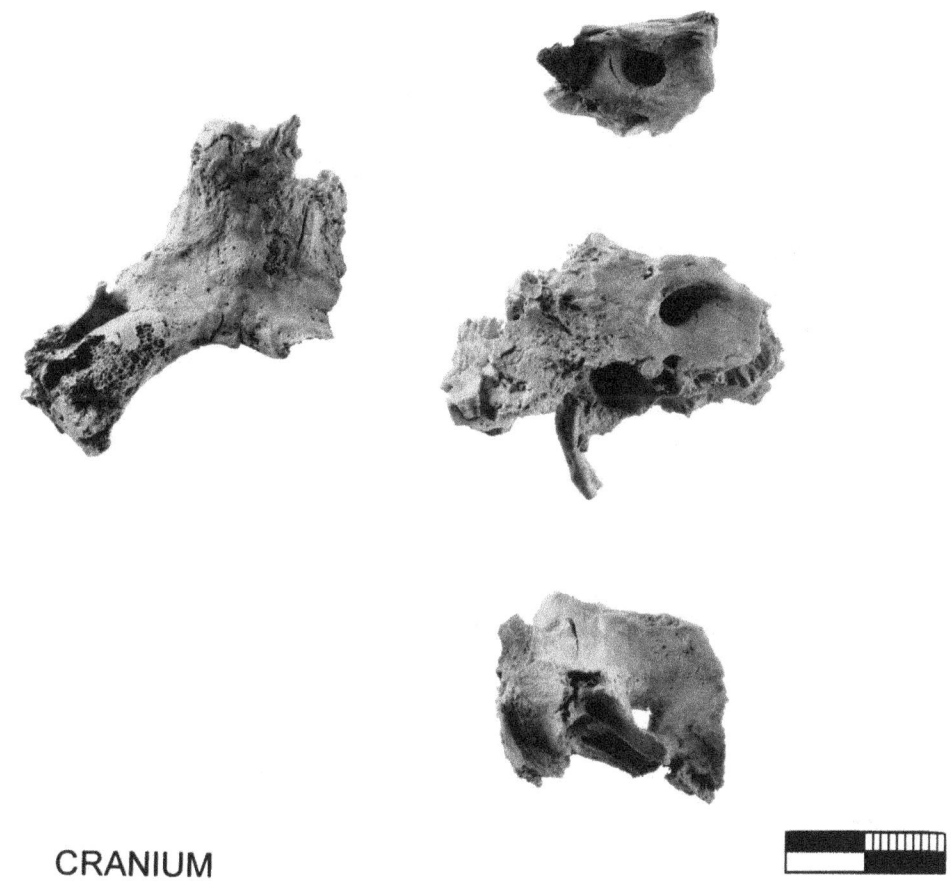

Figure 75. Basi-occipital, petrous and sphenoid bones.

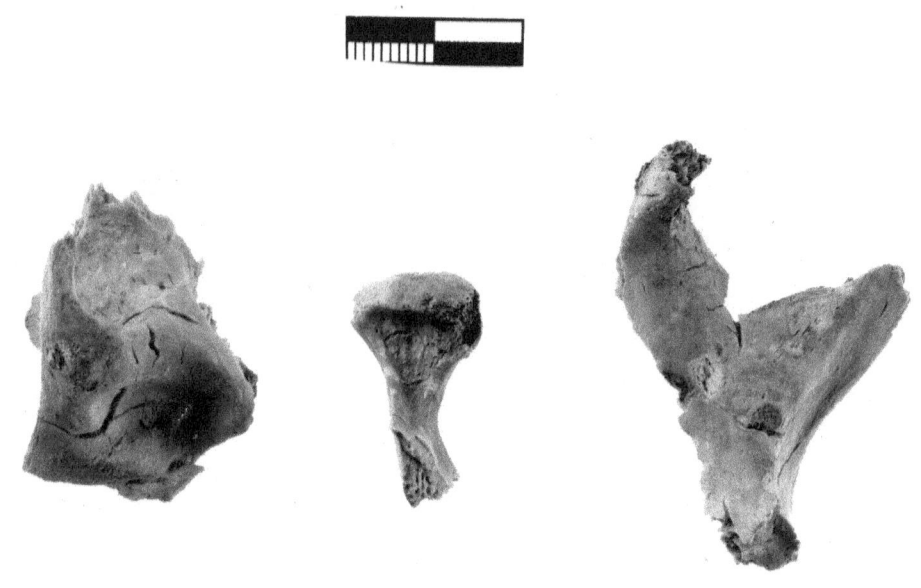

Figure 76. Right temporal and mandible fragments.

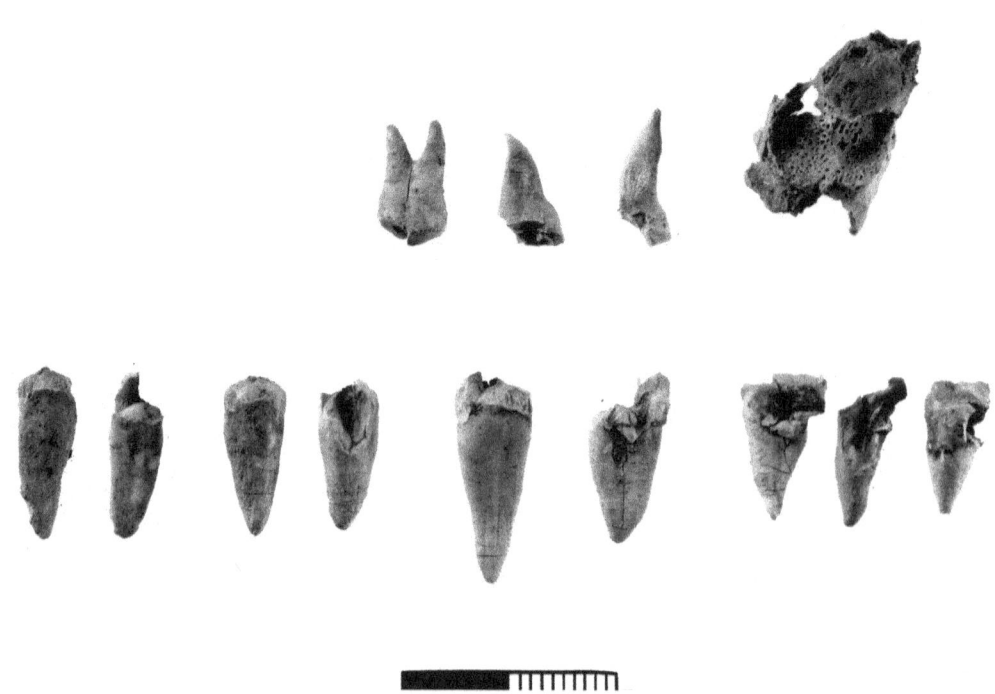

Figure 77. Tooth roots.

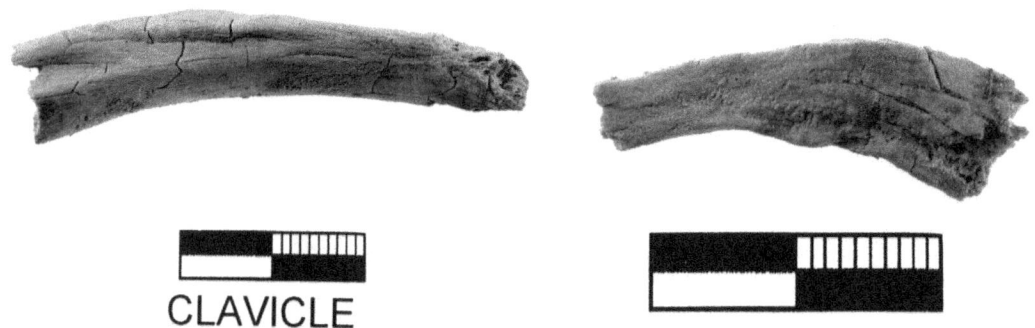

Figure 78. Right clavicle.   **Figure 79.** Left clavicle.

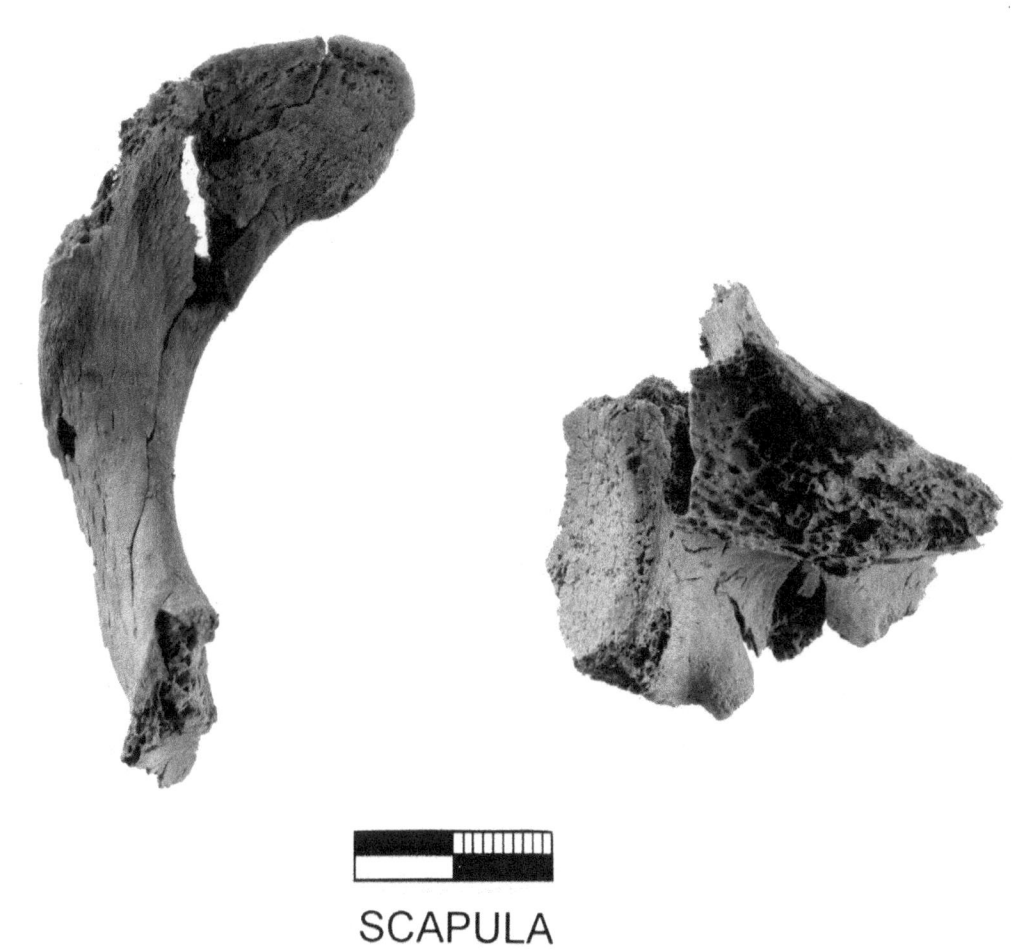

Figure 80. Left scapula fragments.

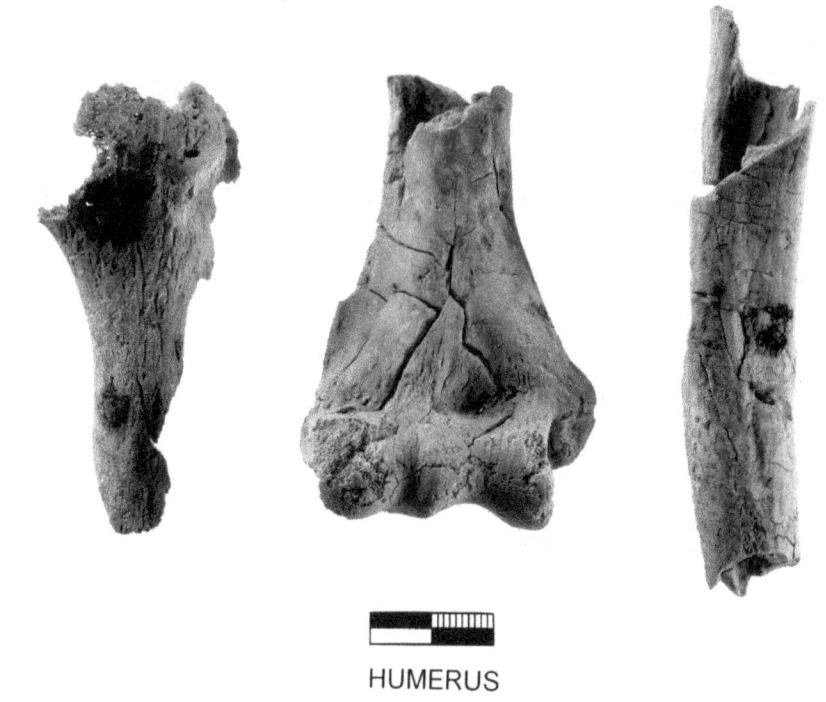

Figure 81. Left and right humerus fragments.

Figure 82. Left humerus.

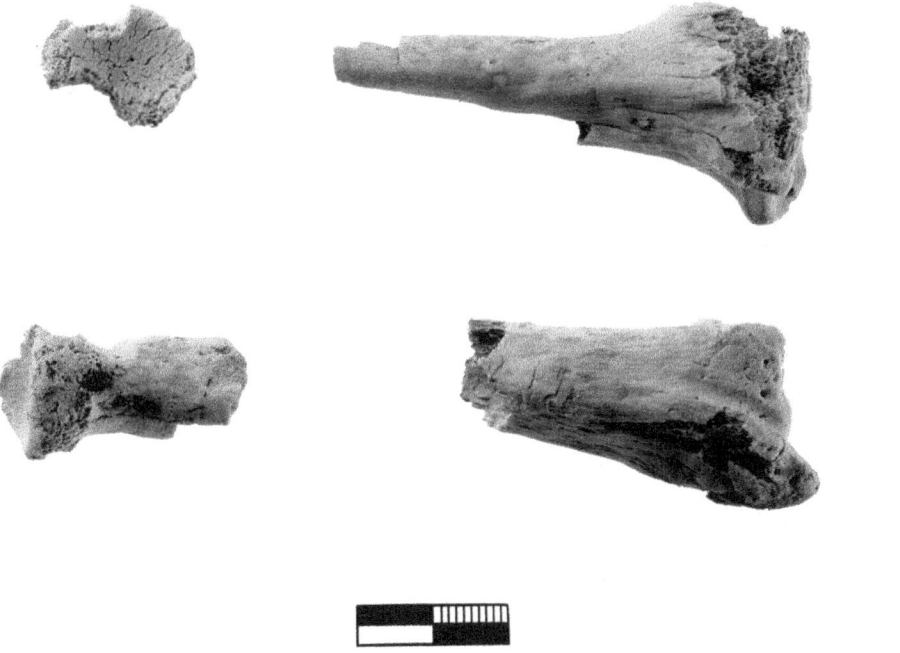

Figure 83. Radiuses.

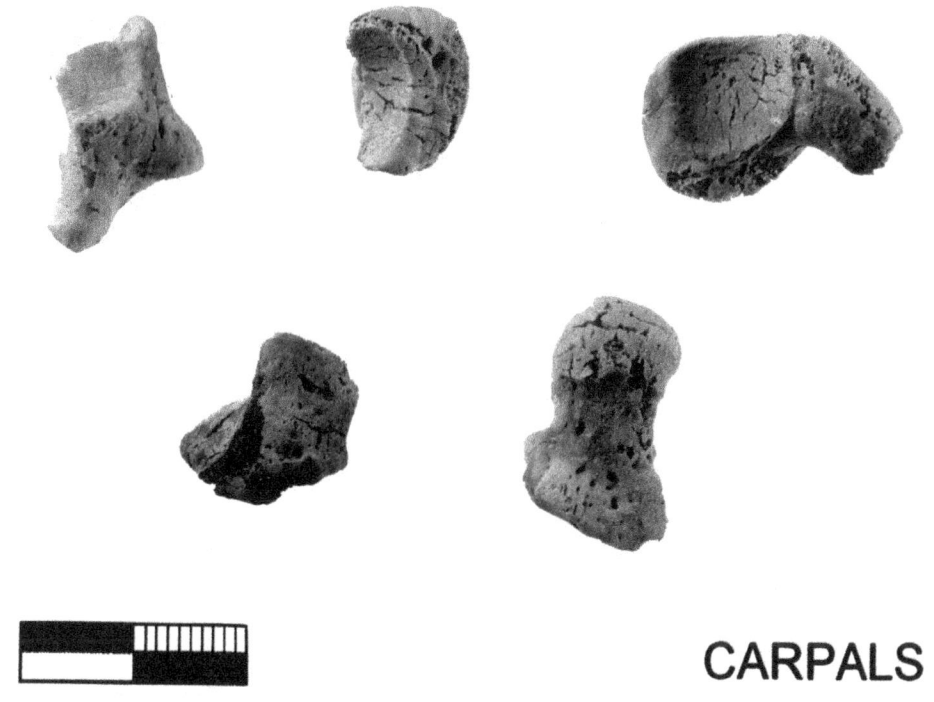

Figure 84. Carpals.

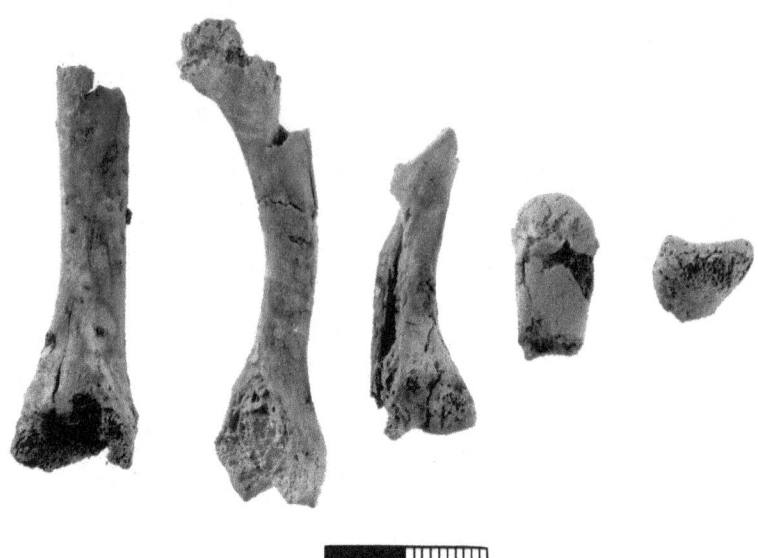

Figure 85. Metacarpals.

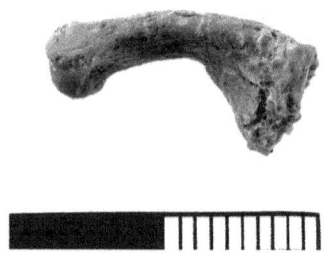

Figure 86. Metacarpal, seriously warped

Figure 87. Phalanges.

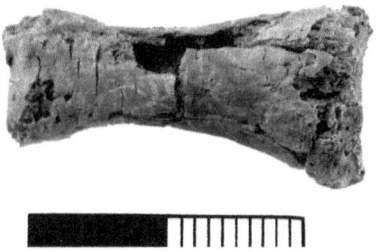

Figure 88. Thumb.

PELVIS

Figure 89. Pelvis and sacrum fragment.

FIBULA   FEMUR

Figure 90. Fibula shaft and femur condyle.

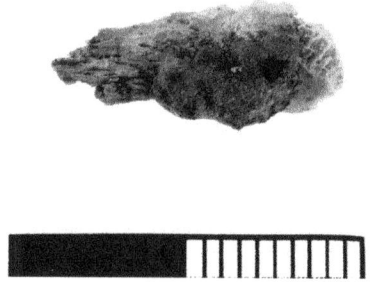

Figure 91. Distal fibula.

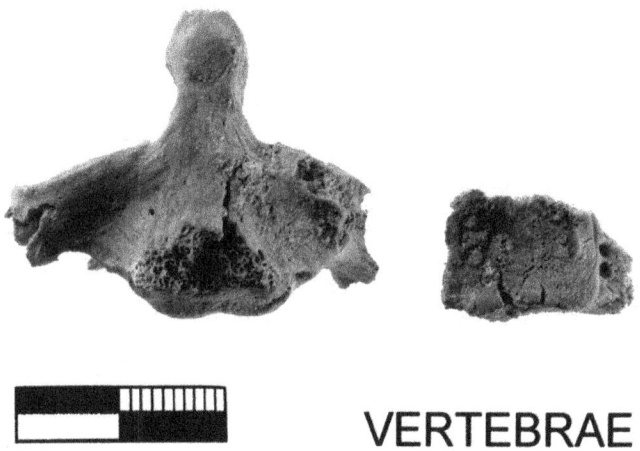

Figure 92. Axis and a cervical body.

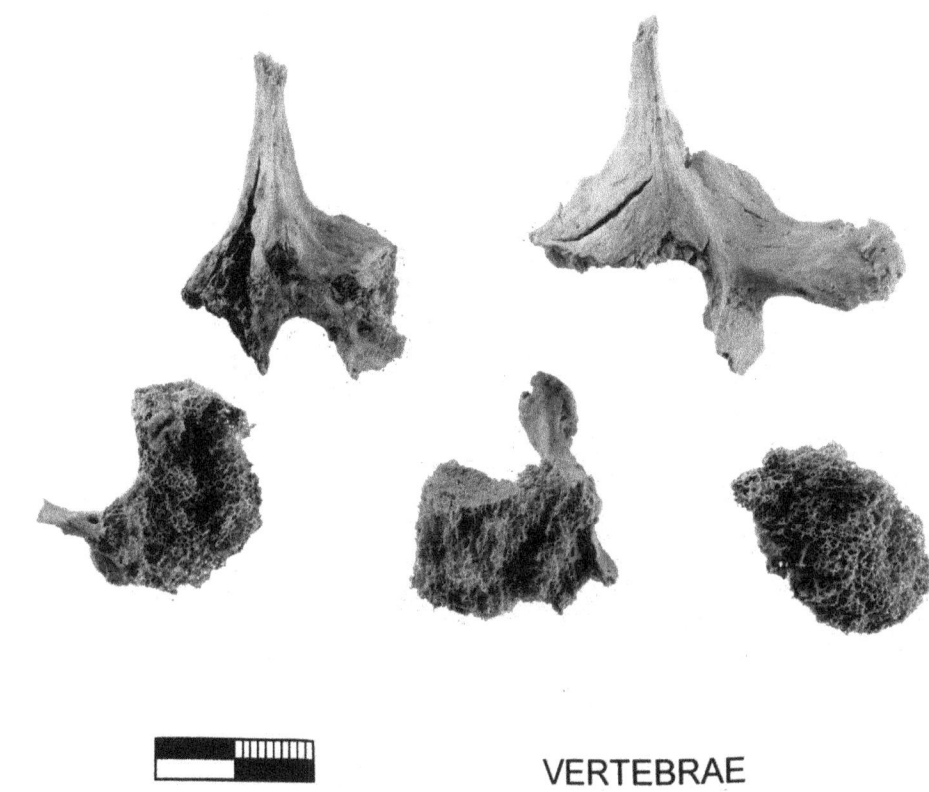

Figure 93. Thoracic fragments.

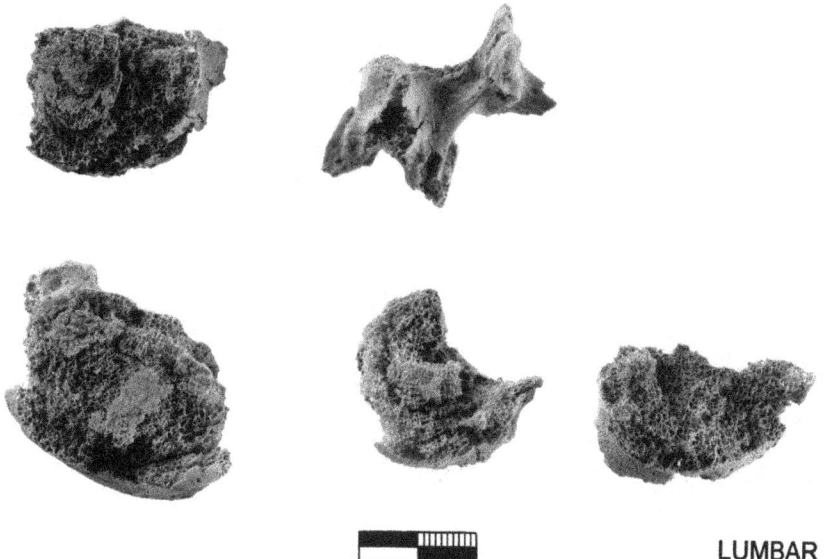

Figure 94. Lumbars.

Figure 95. Lumbar.

Figure 96. Ribs.

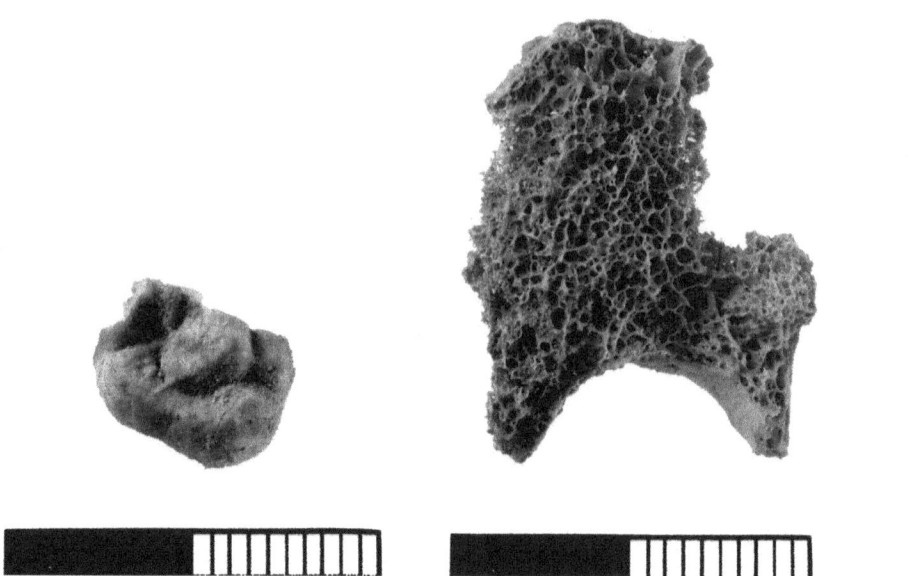

Figure 97. Child's molar.   **Figure 98.** Child's lumbar.

Figure 99. Adult and child lumbars juxtaposed.

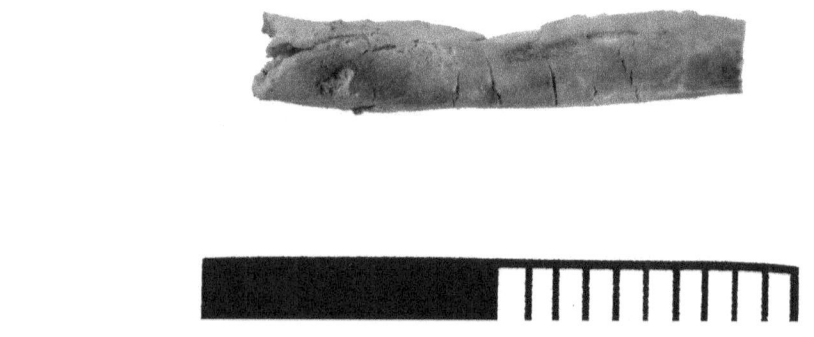

Figure 100. Sheep/goat premolar tooth fragment.

www.ingramcontent.com/pod-product-compliance
Lightning Source LLC
Chambersburg PA
CBHW061544010526
44113CB00023B/2787